T0194699

Jesus Is Not a Genie

My Story: The Prodigal Son Returns

BOB MAXWELL

WestBow Press books may be ordered through booksellers or by contacting:

WestBow Press
A Division of Thomas Nelson & Zondervan
1663 Liberty Drive
Bloomington, IN 47403
www.westbowpress.com
844-714-3454

ISBN: 978-1-6642-2099-7 (sc)
ISBN: 978-1-6642-2100-0 (hc)
ISBN: 978-1-6642-2098-0 (e)

Library of Congress Control Number: 2021901285

Print information available on the last page.

WestBow Press rev. date: 02/09/2021

DEDICATION

First and foremost, I dedicate this book to my Lord and Savior, Jesus Christ; to my God in heaven; and to the Holy Spirit that lives in me.

Second, I dedicate this book to my amazing and Spirit-Filled Mom and Dad, Betty and Jack Maxwell. Thank you, mom and dad, for showing us the Love of Jesus through your loving actions and words. Your joy and happiness are missed but I will be with you again in Heaven one day.

This book is also dedicated to all the prodigal sons and daughters who left the church and turned their backs on God because they felt they were mistreated, talked about, bullied, or judged by Christians and possibly church leaders.

In Luke 15:1–7, Jesus is teaching about the parable of the lost sheep. This is a parable of the prodigal. I was part of the church family and followed Jesus for seventeen years, and then I left the flock—the church, Jesus, and God. I was the lost sheep, and Jesus searched for me for about twenty years until He put me on His shoulders and brought me safely back to His flock.

My prayer is you will find my book an inspiration and a road map to help with your journey back home to God.

This book is dedicated to Christians everywhere with a message to you: it is time to rise up and show the love of Jesus.

Jesus saved me again and welcomed me back into His kingdom and into His loving arms.

He can do the same for you.

Big Jesus hugs.

CONTENTS

ACKNOWLEDGMENTS

There are several pastors who have helped me continue my journey with the Lord. They have inspired me, given me direction, and led me through my spiritual journey through life.

> Without good direction, people lose their way; the more wise counsel you follow, the better your chances. (Proverbs 11:14 MSG)

Rick Warren was my pastor for at least fifteen years at Saddleback Church in Lake Forest, California, and was the most influential person who saved my life and helped me return as a prodigal son to my heavenly Father. Rick is a pastor I can relate to, and I do not feel judged. He made my journey much easier and a lot more fun than I thought it would be. Rick's books and teachings have inspired me and brought me closer to the Lord. I volunteered for several of the community programs Saddleback offered, and I found the heart of Jesus at Saddleback whenever I was on the campus. The classes, the volunteer opportunities to serve, and the opportunities to learn to live and be like Jesus are what Rick and the rest of the pastoral staff talked and walked. I still follow Rick on his daily hope devotional, and when I can, I catch him on his radio program about hope on XM Radio's Family Life Channel, *Pastor Rick's Daily Hope*. I have been following Rick for twenty-five years. I recommitted my life to the Lord in 1996 and was baptized at Saddleback Church on March 26, 2006. (I know: I'm a slow study.)

Greg Laurie is the senior pastor at the Harvest Christian Fellowship in Riverside, California, and leads the Harvest Festivals. Greg holds this event at Angel Stadium each year, and I usually attend. Like Rick Warren, Greg does a great job sharing God's love and teaches how we can use His teachings in our everyday lives. They are very practical teachings. Greg Laurie's morning devotionals are amazing and part of my morning devotions. Greg is a great inspiration and is an important part of my learning to walk with the Lord. During one of Greg's teachings, he mentioned that somebody listening to him had a book the world needed to read in their heart, and I felt a whisper: "This is for you, Bob." I have been following Greg and his teaching for twenty-two years now.

I have been following Joel Osteen, the senior pastor at Lakewood Church in Texas, for the past ten years. I love watching Joel on TV, listening to him on XM Radio, seeing him at his Night of Hope events, and reading his books. Joel inspires me through his encouragement and examples of real people with real lives being changed by God. I listen to Joel's messages several times a day because Joel is like a spiritual fluid keeping me energized. If I did not listen to Joel almost every day on radio or TV, I don't know that I would have had the courage and confidence to write this book.

Jerry Dirmann is the cofounder of the Rock Church in Anaheim, and I decided to change churches and start attending the Rock in November of 2019. I felt that for my ministry, I needed a much deeper understanding of the Bible, and Jerry does a great job breaking down the Bible so it is easier to understand and I am able to apply God's Word in my daily life. Jerry has a daily Bible study on his YouTube channel, where he covers a book in the Bible one chapter a day. I post his daily Bible study on my personal Facebook page and our i-Praise Internet Church Facebook group page. Check it out, and I know you will look at the Bible and God's Word in a different light.

John C. Maxwell is considered the number one business leader in America. John was a pastor of a church for many years before he started his leadership training program. I have followed John since I met him in the mid-1990s. I became a certified trainer and public speaker with the John C. Maxwell organization in 2019.

Thank you to Christian music, XM's The Message, FM's The Fish, and K-Love radio stations! Many times when I am confused or feel the enemy attacking me, I start singing a Christian song out loud or in my mind. If I am afraid, I'll sing "Fear he is a liar" from Zack Brown's hit "Fear Is a Liar."

Turn off secular talk radio stations. Turn on Christian music and Bible-based Christian talk radio so that you are continually getting refilled with the Word of God, the bread of life.

INTRODUCTION

This series of books came to me in a dream. I believe that the Lord placed this dream in my heart, and God wants me to share "Jesus Is Not A Genie" *My Story: The Prodigal Son Returns* and the following series of Jesus Is Not a Genie books to help bring new believers, new followers, millennials, Gen-Xers, and prodigals like myself back to Jesus and to God for the first time.

> For God so loved the world that He gave His only begotten Son, that whoever believes in Him should not perish but have everlasting life. For God did not send His Son into the world to condemn the world, but that the world through Him might be saved. (John 3:16–17 NKJV)

I learned that Jesus is not a genie, and He is not there to pull us out of our messes. But He is always there with His hand reaching out if we will surrender and grab hold of His hand. He will walk beside us and guide us as we walk out the mess we created or are in, always guiding us to our life's purpose.

I pray this book finds a way to encourage you and show you that following Jesus is the safe and secure way to walk out your lives. I pray that you can be yourself, enjoy your walk with the Lord, and not worry about what others think or say or what some religion tells you to believe.

There are millions of stories of people being raised in church and then, like me, being mistreated by the Christian church family with judgment and disapproval. No matter how hard I tried, I could not get away from all the sin they taught me every week.

One week I lied, the next week I drank, the next week I had a lustful thought, and on and on it went!

I finally said, "I've had enough, and if I have to be perfect to follow Jesus, then I don't measure up, and I quit."

This is a story for those of you who have been hurt by religion and religious people who claim to be Christians but act like modern-day Pharisees or Satan in the flesh.

This is a story for those of you who have never heard about God or Jesus and know there must be something better than just sleeping, eating, working, and partying. There must be a purpose for your being alive at this time. I pray that through this book, God will reveal Himself to you, and it will change your life forever.

In this book, I will share my time away from God and how my life was spiraling downward to the point of thinking of suicide because I was so overwhelmed with my drinking and drugs, my marriage falling apart, and thoughts that I would lose my job.

This is a story of God working a miracle in me. God took a broken, lost soul and resurrected me into a strong, God-fearing disciple.

I love Christian music, primarily worship and praise music, and in fact I have always loved singing. I can still remember songs I heard as a kid, even when I have not heard them in thirty years. I can still remember every word, the drumbeats, the guitar licks, and other instruments like I heard them yesterday.

My prayer is that you will remember these songs I write about on your journey, and they will pop into you head when you need them.

One of the first Christian groups I felt connected to was Casting Crowns. The band members of Casting Crowns are also full-time youth pastors, and many of the songs are about struggles the youth were having on a personal basis.

Each chapter of this book has different lines from Christian songs that remind me of how that song helped me in a particular way and at a particular time in my life.

The first chapter is called "My Journey." Check out the song by Casting Crowns called "Nobody." I feel very close to this song, and I can identify with the words. It starts out, "I'm just a nobody, trying to tell everybody." And that is one reason it has taken me over three years to write and publish this book. I did not feel worthy to write it. I am just like every other Christian trying to navigate Christian life. I know there are tens of millions of prodigals in the world.

My prayer is that you will be able to identify in some way with my journey, and that my book may be the light you need on your road back with Jesus by your side.

The Bible says, "For you have delivered me from death and my feet from stumbling, that I may walk before God in the light of life" (Psalm 56:13 NIV).

My prayer is that this book will change your life for the better by helping you move closer to God, Jesus, and the Holy Spirit.

I have never felt so connected to God and so close to Jesus, because I am walking and talking with Him every hour of every day, and my prayer is this book does the same for you.

God bless.

Big Jesus hugs.

One

My Journey

Casting Crowns sings a song called "Nobody," and the words of the song speak to how I've felt many times in my walk back to Jesus.

I've felt like a nobody, and I've been trying to tell everybody I can through one-on-one interactions or group interactions, through my i-Praise Internet Church, on our i-Praise Internet Church group page, and through other social media. But am I qualified? I am not a pastor; I didn't go to seminary or Bible college. My family members aren't pastors, so who do I think I am to go out and tell others about the gospel of Jesus and the salvation we can have because of what Jesus did for us by dying on the cross, taking on all our sins, and rising to heaven to make a place for us?

Have you ever been in the pitch-dark where you were so afraid, where sweat was running down your face and under your arms? Maybe you were running and hiding from the police. Maybe your parents were using drugs or alcohol to self-medicate and were mistreating you. Maybe you were like me, using drugs and alcohol to find a way out of your situation. At least the drugs, loud music, alcohol, and parties numb your mind enough that your problems are stuffed deep down and forgotten for however many hours—until it wears off and you realize the problems haven't changed.

Maybe you are scared to death of being physically and emotionally abused or bullied, not only at school but also at youth programs, young adult programs, or college programs. Abuse doesn't happen because of what you did; it happens because abusers hate themselves so much, and they take it out on you.

That is what bullies do. I am six feet tall and weigh two hundred pounds. I am almost the same size I was when I graduated high school. I played football and was on the wrestling team in high school, but I was bullied in grade school and junior high because my dad was in the military, so I was always the new kid on campus. My sister used to protect me from the kids who bullied me in grade school and elementary, but when I reached junior high, I was on my own. I was kind of chubby as a young kid. I wore the "stocky cut" jeans because I could not fit in skinny jeans, so there were always comments about my looks.

I was also not very good with classroom learning, but I excelled in learning while using my hands, like vocational training classes.

Have you had these problems like I did in school?

I couldn't see the chalkboard because we didn't know I needed glasses until my mom was driving home one day in Long Beach, California, and asked my sister and me if we wanted fries and burgers from a fast food restaurant. In 1964, this restaurant had a huge clown head on a spring, bouncing out of a box like the wind-up toy that was popular at that time, but I could not recognize it. My mom thought I was kidding, but I was not. So at the age of nine I started wearing those handsome black horn-rimmed glasses—aka bully bait! Between my weight, black-rimmed glasses, and being new to the school, the bullies were everywhere.

Because I could not see the chalkboard, I would get bored and talk to someone by me, and that caused me to get in trouble with my teachers.

I was raised in the Baptist church in a very conservative military family. I knew the Ten Commandments and all the punishments of God for my daily sins. At the age of about seventeen, I walked away from God and the church and stayed away from both for about twenty years. I knew I could never measure up to what the pastor, my Sunday school teacher, and my parents told me I had to do if God was going to love me. Man, I sinned within an hour of getting up in the morning, so what was the point? I already felt bad enough about myself and my thoughts and behaviors; I did not need to hear it from other people, especially the people who were supposed to be lifting me up and showing me the love of Jesus. Instead, I was looked down upon, and that made me feel less than and unworthy, like I was a nobody.

I have a bad memory, and we would have to memorize a Bible verse each week. The Sunday school teacher would call on someone to stand and say the memorized verse. I was so afraid that I would be picked to recite the Bible verse by memory that I would get sick to my stomach each week before Sunday school.

I left church and blamed God and Jesus for all my problems and for all my sins. I became like Saul in the book of Acts, persecuting Christians. Not to death like Saul did, but I would make fun of them and taunt them so I could see them get upset and lash out to me. That gave me the opening to say, "Boy, that sure isn't Christlike!" That would get them even more upset, and it gave me more ammunition to go after them and their faith, especially in public.

But one night, I got myself in some real trouble. I had taken acid and was hallucinating while I was trying to drive my truck home. I was dripping with sweat from my head, under my arms, and all over my body. All I knew to do was to grab my Jesus genie bottle, start rubbing the genie bottle, and cry out for help.

Here is the problem: Jesus is not a genie. You cannot kick God and Jesus to the curb, rub the bottle for help when you're in trouble, and expect Jesus to pop out. I am sorry, but at least in my twenty plus years walking with God and Jesus, that is not how I find God works.

First, let me say that Jesus loves all of us! Let me say it again: Jesus loves everybody. Period. There is no changing His mind when we do something wrong, when we relapse, when we stumble, or when we cause problems. Jesus still loves us.

Remember that all that is good is God, and God is good all the time.

After many years away from God, Jesus, and the church, I decided to try a church called Saddleback Church in Lake Forest, California. It was only four miles from my house. A friend knew my background growing up in the church—how I had left and was extremely down on church and Christians in general. My friend told me about this guy Rick Warren and said, "He is different. He doesn't talk like a pastor, he doesn't talk down to you, and he doesn't tell you that you are going to Hades." She said the pastor talked about having a personal relationship with Jesus!

I had to see whether what people were saying about this man Rick Warren and Saddleback Church was true. I will talk about this experience in another chapter in more detail, but I have to say now that Saddleback Church was the first church where I saw the love of Jesus being walked out in people's lives. When I first felt Jesus's love, I wanted to have the type of relationship that Rick and the rest of the pastors shared about each week. In 1996, I recommitted my life to Jesus, accepted Him as my Lord and Savior, asked Him to forgive my sins, and pledged my life to walking with Him. I was water baptized at Saddleback in 2006. Ten years is far too long to wait to be baptized after you receive the Lord as your Savior, but even if you are slow to learn like I am, Jesus still does not discount you or your relationship with Him.

If you have turned away from God for any reason, or if you have never heard of or known God, my prayer is that my story will inspire you and give you a different outlook on your personal relationship with the God who created you and who breathed life into you when you were conceived in your mother's womb.

I once read that there are over 5,467 promises from God to His children in the Bible. One day I am going to start a morning devotional called "God's Daily Promises for Everyone" and share a promise each day to show the love of Jesus.

He is our loving Father in heaven who wants to have the most amazing personal relationship with you. Just you.

The Bible says, "Yet to all who did receive him, to those who believed in his name, he gave the right to become children of God" (John 1:12 NIV).

As I said, I am not a pastor or theologian, and I do not claim to have had any religious instruction in schools of higher learning. But this was true of the disciples of Jesus. They were fishermen, tax collectors, businesspeople, and common people like you and me.

I am speaking through my heart as a disciple of Jesus and through the words of this book, which I believe are inspired by God.

The Bible says in Matthew 28:19–20 (NIV),

> Therefore, go and make disciples of all nations, baptizing them in the name of the Father and of the Son and of the Holy Spirit, and teaching them to obey everything I have commanded you. And surely, I am with you always, to the very end of the age.

This is why the song "Nobody" is so powerful and resonates with me. I felt like a nobody, but God has breathed this book and this ministry in me, and I must share the love of Jesus to everyone who will listen.

In this song, the person is saying to God, "Why did you choose me? Nobody choses me."

Let us stop there for a minute. Have you ever felt like that person in the song?

Someone who is reading this book right now might say, "Oh, my goodness, he is talking about me!" I felt like I was never good enough to be in the cool crowed or the somebodies, like the cheerleaders, band members, and sport jocks. That made me a nobody.

But then there is a turn in awareness with the person! The song lets me know that the *nobodies,* the pushed down, the abused and forgotten—they are the ones God was looking for all the time. He can use me and help me with my ministry.

You see, when you start reading the Bible and studying the people, the stories, and the parables in the Bible, you will find that Jesus liked everyone except the cool religious crowd. Back then they were called the Pharisees. Jesus hated the Pharisees and another "elite religious group" called the Sadducees because they used biblical laws and about two hundred other laws that they came up with to control the Jewish people.

> I have come into the world as a light, so that no one who believes in me should stay in darkness. If anyone hears my words but does not keep them, I do not judge that person. For I did not come to judge the world, but to save the world. (John 12:46–48 NIV)

Jesus loves His children, especially the orphans, the poor, the sick, the widows, the prostitutes, the strippers, the gangbangers, and the tax collectors (which were thought about as badly then as they are today).

Jesus loves you too, no matter where you are on your walk with Him—or maybe you have never met Jesus. I would surely love to introduce Him to you. There will be information in the back of the book where you can contact me, and I would love to hear your story.

I felt like I was not even qualified to think I could write a book people would want to read and share with their families and friends.

I thought, "I want to tell the world all the wonderful things God has done and continues to do in my life, but I'm not qualified. I'm just a nobody."

Have you ever felt like this before? You believe in your heart and soul that you found your purpose, and as you tell family and friends, they feel it's their purpose to play God and redefine your purpose for you!

My suggestion is to keep it to yourself until you are able to figure out enough to start walking in your purpose. When people say, "Why do you do that now?" you can say, "It's a part of my purpose, and I have started my personal walk with Jesus. He is leading my way."

What can they say? Do you think they would ever say, "Don't walk or follow Jesus?" No way!

We are all marked as Christians to go out into the world and share the love of Jesus and salvation into heaven.

The Great Commission

> Then the eleven disciples went to Galilee, to the mountain where Jesus had told them to go. When they saw him, they worshiped him; but some doubted. Then Jesus came to them and said, "All authority in heaven and on earth has been given to me. Therefore go and make disciples of all nations, baptizing them in the name of the Father and of the Son and of the Holy Spirit, and teaching them to obey everything I have commanded you. And surely, I am with you always, to the very end of the age. (Matthew 28:16–20 NIV)

The Greatest Commandment

> Hearing that Jesus had silenced the Sadducees, the Pharisees got together. One of them, an expert in the law, tested him with this question: "Teacher, which is the greatest commandment in the Law?"

> Jesus replied: "'Love the Lord your God with all your heart and with all your soul and with all your mind.' This is the first and greatest commandment. And the second is like it: 'Love your neighbor as yourself.' All the Law and the Prophets hang on these two commandments." (Matthew 22:36–40 MSG)

"Jesus Is Not A Genie" *My Story: The Prodigal Son Returns* is about being raised Baptist from birth to late teens, leaving God and the church for over twenty years, and my return to my Father Jesus Christ as His prodigal son.

My prayer is that this book will inspire you to come back to the Lord and start a new relationship with Him. My prayer is if you are walking with the Lord now, you will find a deeper relationship with Him while reading this book. If you never had a relationship or have never accepted Jesus into your life, I pray this book will help you start your new journey. I pray we can help you walk out that journey together, because we do not have to have this figured out completely before we start walking with Jesus, and every day is a new day. Amen.

I look forward to hearing from you and how this book has helped you return to the Father, find a deeper relationship with our heavenly Father, and discover how He brought out joy, peace, love, hope, acceptance, and abundance into your life, your business or workplace, and your family's lives.

I want to welcome anyone who wants to receive the Lord while reading this book to read a prayer I will have within some chapters and at the end of the book to help you come to the Lord, receive Him as your Savior, ask Him to forgive your sins, and promise to follow Him forever, amen.

As Joel Osteen always says, "Your life will never be the same again."

> Therefore, if anyone is in Christ, he is a new creation. The old has passed away; behold, the new has come. (2 Corinthians 5:17 ESV)

Is it time to come back to God? Is it time to accept Jesus as your Savior? Now is a great time. Stop reading for a moment and say, "Dear Jesus, I need You in my life. I repent of my sins, Father. I accept You as my Lord and Savior for the rest of my life. I surrender my heart and my life to You. Reveal Yourself to me and through me, in Jesus's Name."

By saying and believing these words, you have been born again! Congratulations, and welcome to our family! We are so proud of you.

Check out our website at www.i-Praise.org, which is the Internet church I founded and launched on Easter Sunday 2019 with five people, called i-Praise Internet Church. As of this writing one year later, we have grown to over 1,500 people who follow us on our group page on Facebook. I share messages as God leads me, and we share the different ministries we support. I pray you will join us and become part of our i-Praise Internet Church family.

NOTES

Two

The Prodigal Son Returns

The Bible tells the story of the prodigal son.

This very rich man had two sons, and one day the younger son told his father he was leaving home. He was heading out on his own, so he asked for his father's inheritance to finance his new life. The father gave the son his portion, and the son left. But the son made several poor choices: drinking, chasing wild women, and squandering all his inheritance. Sounds like me, but without the inheritance!

He finally had to find a job working to make a living, but a famine came, and the only work was slopping the pigs.

One day, he came to his senses and returned to his father.

> When he finally came to his senses, he said to himself, "At home even the hired men have food enough and to spare, and here I am, dying of hunger! I will go home to my father and say, 'Father, I have sinned against both heaven and you, and am no longer worthy of being called your son. Please take me on as a hired man.'"

> So, he returned home to his father. And while he was still a long distance away, his father saw him coming, and was filled with loving pity and ran and embraced him and kissed him. (Luke 15:17–20 TLB)

The Bible goes on the say in Luke 15:22–24 (NIV),

> But the father said to his servants, "Quick! Bring the best robe and put it on him. Put a ring on his finger and sandals on his feet. Bring the fattened calf and kill it. Let's have a feast and celebrate. For this son of mine was dead and is alive again; he was lost and is found." So they began to celebrate.

What have you run away from, God or your parents? The story continues as they began to celebrate.

> Meanwhile, the older son was in the field. When he came near the house, he heard music and dancing. He called one of the servants and asked him what was going on. "Your brother has come," he replied, "and your father has killed the fattened calf because he has him back safe and sound."
>
> The older brother became angry and refused to go in. His father went out and pleaded with him. But he answered his father, "Look! All these years I've been slaving for you and never disobeyed your orders. Yet you never gave me even a young goat so I could celebrate with my friends. But when this son of yours who has squandered your property with prostitutes comes home, you kill the fattened calf for him!"

> "My son," the father said, "you are always with me, and everything I have is yours. But we had to celebrate and be glad, because this brother of yours was dead and is alive again; he was lost and is found." (Luke 15:24–32 NIV)

Jesus is sharing in this parable about the prodigal son that even when we run away from Him, even when we blow everything, Jesus is our heavenly Father, and He can't wait until we return to Him. He will come running to us with open arms and no judgment or damnation!

I ran from the church, but in doing so, I ran away from my heavenly Father. I blamed Jesus and thought badly of Him because of how His so-called Christian followers behaved and treated me. I thought, These Christian's are not following the teachings of the Bible, and they are treating me badly, talking behind my back, and telling me what a sinner I am. I said to myself, If Jesus loves this accuser, I do not want anything to do with Jesus. I blamed every negative thing that happened to me—which was 90 percent my fault—on Jesus and God. I stayed away from church for about twenty years.

Are you like me? Did you leave the church to try to do life on your own? Is your life like the story of the prodigal son?

How is that working for you?

My fellow Christian brothers and sisters, we must do what we can to stop sex trafficking, unwanted teen pregnancy, and selective aborting of unborn human beings. Can we stop the verbal chatter, political positioning, and the "money over people" society we live in? We need to become a country of civility, compassion, kindness, hand up, and pay it forward. We must not forget where we came from.

We need to get back to what the Bible says about treating our neighbors as ourselves.

One of the things I have learned is that if we do not believe or follow Jesus, we are in a boat without a rudder. We aimlessly drift from place to place, job to job, and relationship to relationship, floating around and trying to find a solid foundation, trying to find the next thing we think will give us the joy and peace we are craving.

But if we finally surrender to the Source that breathed life into us when we were formed in our mothers' wombs, and if we make God our final thing, He will give us everything we need, and God can never lie; only Satan and people lie.

I would get in trouble and pull out my "Jesus Genie." I'd pray, "Please, Jesus, I need Your help. If You help me out of this mess, I promise to follow You." If He did not rescue me as soon as the words fell off my tongue, I was cursing Him. But I learned quickly Jesus is not a genie.

Only when we get in trouble do we call on Jesus to get us out of the mess we are in and make Him so many promises as "payments."

The Bible says that we will walk through the valley, and God, our Daddy, is there waiting for us to walk through the valley with Him, hand in hand with Jesus.

Like me, when many people leave the church, they also leave their relationship with Jesus and God, and that is an eternal shame. But when I looked back, it was not Jesus who let me down; it was myself and immature Christians. I have learned not to put my trust in people and only to put my trust in God.

God's Word teaches us a lot through what are called parables, but what is a parable?

Merriam-Webster's Dictionary defines a parable as "a usually short fictitious story that illustrates a moral attitude or a religious principle."

So how do we break down this story or parable, and how does it pertain to our lives today?

This story about the prodigal son is a parable for us to see how much love God has for us.

What are you running away from? Are you running from your earthly family, your spouse, yourself, your heavenly Father, Jesus, the church, reality, responsibility, or the authorities, just to name a few?

I was running from the police at times, Jesus, the church, and my family. I just wanted to work and party. But like the young son in the story, I was so desperate that I would either die or humble myself before Jesus. I finally said, "I give up, Jesus. I cannot do this on my own."

I asked Jesus for forgiveness for all my sins, and I acknowledge God is the Father, Jesus is the Son, and the Holy Spirit lives in me. In 1996, I rededicated my life to God. In 2006, I was baptized at Saddleback Church, showing publicly that I chose Jesus as my Lord and Savior.

Is it time in your life to humble yourself in front of the Lord, get back down on your knees, repent, and ask for forgiveness?

Is it time for you to come home and make it right with your family and friends?

Is it time you committed or recommitted your life to Jesus?

God is saying to us in John 14:3 (NIV), And if I go and prepare a place for you, I will come back and take you to be with me that you also may be where I am."

I can imagine how tough this was for this young man, having to go home and face his family and friends. People might say, "Yeah, here comes the big man, the guy who told us he was moving away and would make a name for himself."

The young man basically said, "I don't need my father. I am the man of my own life." But now he is desperate, so he knows he must humble himself before his earthly father.

We see Dad is on the porch rocking away, just waiting for the day his young son will return to him. Off in a distance, he thinks he sees someone coming toward him. Finally, he recognizes it is his young son, and he takes off running toward him.

Once he makes contact with the young son, he hugs him tight and welcomes him home. The son had a speech ready for his dad.

> And the son said to him, Father, I have sinned against heaven and in your sight; I am no longer worthy to be called your son. (Luke 15:21 NASB)

Have you messed up like me, and do you have your speech ready?

In these cases, we find out that Jesus is not a genie. He will not magically remove us from a situation. He can, because He's God, but He will not in most cases. He will not abandon you like people will, but Jesus is not a genie. He will give us a hand up, and He will show us the path to living a fulfilled life, but He will not drag us along our path.

The Bible says in Isaiah 41:10 (NIV), "So do not fear, for I am with you; do not be dismayed, for I am your God. I will strengthen you and help you; I will uphold you with my righteous right hand."

We must understand a few things that Jesus was trying to illustrate in this parable. In those days, in that culture, Jewish fathers did not run anywhere or to anyone. It would be considered a very disrespectful action, so I feel the father is saying by his actions, "I don't care if I am embarrassed by running to you. I love you so much, I am willing to be ridiculed by the world views just so I can get to you as fast as possible."

Remember, the young man was in a pigpen, so you know what he smelled like and looked like, but his father couldn't care less. The Bible says, "He ran to his son, threw his arms around him and kissed him." Luke 15:20 (NIV)

> But the father said to his servants, "Quick! Bring the best robe and put it on him. Put a ring on his finger and sandals on his feet. Bring the fattened calf and kill it. Let's have a feast and celebrate. For this son of mine was dead and is alive again; he was lost and is found." So they began to celebrate. (Luke 15:22–24 NIV)

Did you know that Jesus wants a full-blown loving relationship with you exactly where you are at, no matter what you look like or smell like? It is true!

We pick up the story with the young man's confession to his father, and I can just hear his father being surprised by the young man and what he might be saying. "Are you kidding me? You are my son. You have my blood running through your veins."

The dad tells one of his employees to bring a beautiful robe and a ring for his young son to wear, and to get a young fat calf slaughtered so they can start a "welcome home" party.

The son represents people like me, I had left the church and gone out partying, becoming very sinful. I wasted so much money and time trying to find something or someone who could fill my needs and desires, but that can be filled only with Jesus's love because God put that in our "GNA" (God's natural anointing).

In the end, all I had were huge bills, little to no friends, zero good friends or relationships, no direction, and no hope as to what was happening in my life or my future.

Now, when I say God, Jesus, and the Holy Spirit speak to me, I don't mean audibly. Most of the time for me, it is in a dream state, a vision, or a revealing thought. As I go to sleep, I am thanking the Lord for my day and having a conversation with my Friend and Father Jesus Christ about my day. I am thanking Him for anything and everything that went well, and I ask for His wisdom, grace, and mercy on what might not be going well. I recommend this to everyone. Jesus is the last thought in your mind, and now the Holy Spirit can go to work in you, giving you dreams, ideas, thoughts, solutions to problems, and more. Try it every night for thirty days. The very last thing you think about as you are falling asleep is thanking and praising Jesus. It will become a habit, and you will never go to sleep any other way.

I also hear God speaking to me through music with certain artists and groups, I feel most deeply connected with their lyrics.

During that sleep state, I get visions of myself doing different things, like sitting at a desk writing this book. It was not all the time and not every night. That would be super cool if I felt or saw God's presence every night when I sleep, but the Bible does not say God comes to even the most mature believer every night.

When I first wake up in the morning and open my eyes, I start to sing a blessing to Jesus: "I Love You, Lord." We were taught this song at the Vineyard of Anaheim Church I attended after Saddleback. There are some very beautiful renditions of this song on YouTube. I have turned this into my night's prayer to God. "I love you Lord, and I lift my voice, to worship you and my soul rejoices. I pray that You take joy Jesus, in what You hear from my voice and may it be a sweet sound in Your ear, amen."

I lie still and wait on my friend Jesus. Sometimes I lie there for about five minutes, and if I do not get any kind of feeling in my heart or in my soul, then I simply thank God for whatever He has planned for me. I might sing a Christian song in my head, get up, and get ready for my day.

I start my day with daily devotions and reading my Bible. When I read verses in my Bible, I try to share the words that touch me, usually to our i-Praise Internet Church group page on Facebook or the guys at my business.

If I am lying there resting on the Lord, and an idea pops in my head or deeper in my soul, I get a stirring, an action feeling. Then I know the Lord is confirming my dream. If I remember the dream when I wake up, Jesus confirms that by giving me those inner feelings, I know it is time to put the dream into action of some sort.

Have you ever been sleeping, resting, or doing yoga, and an idea or feeling comes from inside you—a thought, an intuition, an impression? That is God speaking to you through the Holy Spirit. That is Jesus filling your spirit with whatever He wants you to hear. God talks to us all the time. Some people say they hear from God through their intuitions.

Dr. Wayne Dyer was a teacher of connecting our souls to the Source. He was not a pastor, but his teachings were very spiritual. I loved listening to him speak and reading his books. He died several years ago, but I still like to remember some of his quotes that inspired me, such as "Change the way you look at things and the things you look at change." That could be a four-week teaching message on our i-Praise Internet Church website.

The Lord doesn't care about the mistakes you and I have made; He loves us unconditionally. Jesus wants a true and living relationship with you. Jesus teaches us to follow Him, learn from Him, and teach His Word to others.

Feel Him holding you and comforting you with His loving arms wrapped around you, and then you go hold and comfort someone else. He will give you riches beyond your belief, an amazing family, good health, and wonderful abundance. Take what you are given and give what Jesus has given you to others so they can see the glory of the Lord through your kindness and goodness. God will reward you in heaven when you go home to Jesus and our Father, God.

> The Bible says in 1 John 1:8–10 (MSG),
>
> If we claim that we're free of sin, we're only fooling ourselves. A claim like that is errant nonsense. On the other hand, if we admit our sins—make a clean breast of them—he won't let us down; he'll be true to himself. He'll forgive our sins and purge us of all wrongdoing. If we claim that we've never sinned, we out-and-out contradict God—make a liar out of him. A claim like that only shows off our ignorance of God.

It is so hard yet so worth it to follow Jesus. You might need a mentor and some friends to help you get started. Check me out on my i-Praise Internet Church website, www.i-Praise.org; our i-Praise Facebook group page; and on our i-Praise YouTube channel. I would love to connect with people checking out the God and this Jesus thing. Maybe you need prayer or some scripture to meditate on. Please reach out to me and our i-Praise team.

As a prodigal son, returning to my Father in heaven has been such a wild ride filled with more ups and downs that I ever could imagine, but I have never been so happy, content, and excited about what God has in store for me.

Are you a prodigal child who was hurt by other Christians, so you turned your back on Jesus like I did? Is it time for you to give God another chance in your life?

NOTES

Three

My Friend Jesus

One of the songs by Casting Crowns that really hit home with me is called "Who Am I."

The Bible says in Ephesians 2:8–9 (NIV),

> For it is by grace you have been saved, through faith—and this is not from yourselves, it is the gift of God—not by works, so that no one can boast.

The song says to me, "Who am I that the Lord would care to know me. Why would He be interested in how I feel, how I hurt, and what I have done? Why would the God of the universe, who claims to know my name and the other billions of people on earth, care to help me? His Word says that He will comfort me, protect me, and love me unconditionally.

When I hurt inside or out, God hurts along with me? Really? Why?

This is why, and this is from our God, our Abba Father: Before I formed you in the womb, I knew you, And before you were born I consecrated you; I have appointed you a prophet to the nations. (Jeremiah 1:5 NASB)

I understand the word *consecrate* means to make something sacred or to make a statement about someone or something that is sacred.

To me, we can read this verse like this: before we were conceived, God already knew us, what we would look like, what our purpose would be, and even when we will die. Before we were a twinkle in our parents' eyes, God knew everything about us. I thought this was mind-blowing until I thought of the universe and how big and vast it is. I heard recently that some well-known astronomers triangulated three massive telescopes, in three parts of the world, so they could magnify their individual strength, and combined they could see many galaxies farther away from Earth than ever before. They were amazed when the found one hundred billion galaxies and two hundred billion stars, on average, per galaxy.

> And God made two great lights; the greater light to rule the day, and the lesser light to rule the night: he made the stars also. (Genesis 1:16 KJV)

Some of the Bible verses, stories, and parables that are in my book and of course in the Bible might sounds at times far out of reality or possibility. You must decide whether or not you believe the Bible.

Many Christians want to pick and choose what parts of the Bible they believe and what parts they feel have room for their personal interpretations, like the Pharisees in Jesus's day.

Why do you think we have so many religious groups, denominations, and subgroups of certain groups or denominations? They interpret the Bible so it fits their worldly environment, trying to grow their church size and popularity for personal fame and fortune instead of teaching right out of the Bible. They should teach exactly what God's Word says—nothing more or less.

One of the greatest pastors I have had the privilege to be taught the Bible by is the pastor of my home church, Pastor Jerry Dirmann, senior pastor and cofounder of the Rock Church in Anaheim, California, with his anointed wife, Kimberly. Jerry teaches right out of the Bible, word for word—no deviation, no personal opinions, just the Word of God speaking through Jerry and to his students.

I heard about the Rock, Anaheim, and Pastor Jerry from a friend I trusted. Because I never went to Bible college or seminary, I felt ill-equipped to minister to people about my Faith and the Gospel because I didn't feel I understood enough about the Bible and how to explain it to others. I changed churches and became a member of the Rock. I have learned so much and am thankful to Jerry, Kimberly, and the rest of the Rock family.

We read again in Jeremiah 1:5 (NASB), "Before I formed you in the womb, I knew you, And before you were born I consecrated you; I have appointed you a prophet to the nations." It's sounds impossible, but I have heard, seen, and experienced things that have happened to me and others, and these things could only have been because there is a good God watching over us—watching over more than seven billion people at the same time. Wow, nothing is impossible for God, Jesus, and the Holy Spirit. Simply believe and have faith the size of a mustard seed, and God will make you into an orchard of faith.

When I left the church and God at age seventeen, I felt like God, Jesus, and the Holy Spirit did not love me or even care about me because I was such a mess. "You are such a sinner," as my Sunday School teacher would tell me every Sunday.

I knew in my heart that I was rebelling against any authority that wanted to tell me how I should live my life. I was so tired of having all my weak points magnified.

My sister was very smart in school, and I was not—and every report card, I was reminded of it. I would get sick to my stomach when report cards were issued. I knew when my dad saw mine, I would be in big trouble, and I would be compared to my smarter sister. My mom was always trying to make me feel better by calmly talking to me about studying more, asking more questions in class, and asking for help from my teacher.

Yeah, right! I hated studying, and I was told I needed to study more? Ask questions in class? Really? Do you know how brutal kids can be when you raise your hand and ask a question everybody else knows the answer to except you? Stay after class and get help from the teacher? Are you kidding me? I wanted out of there as soon as the last bell rang!

Can you relate to my problems in school? Did you have a tough time in school, or did you have a sibling to whom school came easily? How did you feel when report cards were handed out?

As soon as I turned eighteen, I moved out of my parents' house and was going to be a millionaire by age thirty. I was going to show everyone I knew how I did not need good grades and did not need to go to college to be successful. I did not need God or anyone else telling me to slow down and be careful of where I was headed. I knew, or thought I knew, how the world worked and how I was going to take shortcuts to my success and riches. Does this sound like the parable of the lost son from a previous chapter? That was me!

What I did not know was how little I knew about this mean, tough, and unforgiving world in which we live. I continually made financial mistakes, as well as mistakes living with roommates (always males). I was jumping from job to job for instant gratification and not planning my future.

> My sheep hear My voice, and I know them, and they follow Me. (John 10:27 NIV)

Jesus was calling for me to come back home, but I was too hardheaded to respond. In another chapter, I will share the parable of the lost sheep and the lost coin.

At the age of twenty-two, I married for the first time. We were both cosmetology students—yes, I was a hairstylist—and after fifteen months in school and successfully passing our Arizona State cosmetology test, we were licensed and ready to set the world on fire! We moved in together, and both of us went to work for a couple of different shop owners over the first year. In year two, I decided to open our first shop, a little four-chair shop in a medical center right next to a big hospital. In year three, we bought a twelve-chair shop a few miles away.

Unfortunately, the marriage did not last, and after five years we divorced.

Now remember, I left the church and stopped believing there was a God, but as was my history, whenever I or my marriage needed immediate fixing, I'd grab my Jesus Genie and rub away, crying out to Jesus to get me out of the particular mess. But Jesus is not a genie, and I was not doing my part as a follower. I was being a user of Jesus, not a follower or believer.

What a devastating time in my life, and it did not seem like my "million dollars by thirty" program was going to happen. I have always been a very positive, focused person, so I thought thirty might be too soon, but by forty it would happen. Let me fast-forward for you on my millionaire journey. I am sixty-five years old and still not a millionaire!

I had enough Christian teachings to know a little of God's promises, so I would grab my Jesus Genie and start rubbing and "praying," making all my promises. But Jesus is not a genie, and He is not going to answer every prayer for us instantly. Therefore, I would get mad at God and say, "See? I knew You weren't real!"

I sold that business to go into business with my father selling and servicing lawn and garden machines, as well as construction equipment like generators, cement finishers, cement mixers, and asphalt tampers, to name a few.

It had been about two years since my divorce before I remarried, and was married for twenty-seven years, raising two children she had had with two previous husbands. I was heavy into drinking every night and smoking pot while irresponsibly raising two children. Our son was eight, and our daughter was two when we married.

I was not a bad person, but I made bad choices. I was responsible, buying a house and always having good jobs. I paid our bills on time and thought I was living the American dream. But this behavior carried on for seventeen to twenty years of our marriage. We never went to church or talked about God in a positive way; we were 100 percent about us.

Did you ever do anything you deeply regret when you were raising your kids?

The year was 1995, and I was working for Sam's Club in southern California. I had a wonderful boss who was also a very good friend, and she knew my past experience with Christians and church. She and her husband had started attending Saddleback Church in Lake Forest, California. They had met Pastor Rick Warren, and she said she thought I would enjoy his teachings. The church sanctuary had recently been built, and Saddleback was expanding quickly.

I started attending Saddleback every Sunday, but I could not get my wife to go with me. She knew my past and said, "God doesn't want anything to do with you. You drink and party during the week, and then you go to church on Sunday? You hypocrite!"

Do you think God expects you to be perfect before He will have anything to do with you?

> If we claim that we're free of sin, we're only fooling ourselves. A claim like that is errant nonsense. On the other hand, if we admit our sins—make a clean breast of them—he won't let us down; he'll be true to himself. He'll forgive our sins and purge us of all wrongdoing. If we claim that we've never sinned, we out-and-out contradict God—make a liar out of him. A claim like that only shows off our ignorance of God. (1 John 1:8–10 MSG)

I kept attending Saddleback even though she kept making fun of me, calling me Christian Boy and Jesus Lover. I sat all the way in the back of the church just in case I needed a quick exit, or in case Rick or another pastor looked over and saw me. It is amazing how Satan works in our heads and through friends and family to make us feel that Jesus is not for us. Satan made me feel like I had to have it all together if I were going to be a Christian, and I had better not stumble over my sin and bad behavior because Jesus would cut me off, and then where would I be?

It was not an easy journey back, but I listened to Rick and his message of the love of Jesus. He said it's OK if you make a mistake, stumble over sin, and take two steps forward and one step back as long as you take two more steps forward and then three, and then five, and then twenty. Even if you fall by five or ten steps, you can get up, dust yourself off, ask Jesus to forgive you, and start moving forward again.

I embraced all of what Saddleback was teaching, and I started tithing a little. Baby steps, right? I started taking all their classes and joined in the outreach programs Saddleback offered. I started attending the Wednesday night worship and spent a lot of time praying in a garden area by the sanctuary.

> Therefore, if anyone is in Christ, he is a new creation. The old has passed away; behold, the new has come. All this is from God, who through Christ reconciled us to himself and gave us the ministry of reconciliation; that is, in Christ, God was reconciling the world to himself, not counting their trespasses against them, and entrusting to us the message of reconciliation. Therefore, we are ambassadors for Christ, God making his appeal through us. We implore you on behalf of Christ, be reconciled to God. (2 Corinthians 5:17–20 ESV)

The Bible is the inspired Word of God sent through prophets and disciples. When we read the Bible, we cannot read it like a novel or biography. Each book and chapter stands alone and can refer to other books and chapters between the Old Testament and the New Testament.

I joined a small group for Bible study, but they were so far ahead of me in their knowledge of the Bible that I felt like when I was in school. The smart ones knew the answers, and dumb Bob did not know anything. Therefore I left and never joined another small group until around 2010.

Did anybody else feel that way when first walking with God or returning to God like I was?

I went to The Harvest Crusades and heard Pastor Greg Laurie for the first time, and I was blown away. He teaches a lot like Pastor Rick, so I was really drawn into Pastor Greg's message on the Gospel of Jesus Christ. Greg teaches right out of the Bible but made it relevant to the life I was living, so I started following Greg on the Internet through his website, and I also started his daily devotions, which I still do every morning.

My life at home continued to get worse, to the point where I ate before I came home, went to the garden area at Saddleback, and prayed for a while before heading to the house. When I arrived, I went right up to my bedroom and stayed there until it was time to get up and go to work the next day. This went on for almost ten years.

Now I was a dedicated follower of Jesus, and I thought rubbing my Jesus genie bottle should work and solve my problems. But again, Jesus is not a genie, and not all my prayers were answered immediately or at all, if my pray request was not in alignment with God's plan for my future, my purpose.

I decided to stop listening to sports talk radio, which was on in my car twenty-four seven. I decided to start listening to Christian music whenever I was in my car. I found two nationally syndicated FM stations, The Fish and K-Love Radio, which you can find across America.

I started worshiping in my car, but at the time I did not know that was what I was doing. Because I have always loved music, singing felt natural. As I learned the songs, I remembered the words. To this day, I still have trouble memorizing Bible verses. I remember the scripture and the content, but trying to remember where I read it is hard for me. But remembering the words to a song? I can do that very easily.

I would get in my car and start singing music by Casting Crowns, Jeremey Riddle, Jeremy Camp, Natalie Grant, Bethel Music, Hillsong, Michael W. Smith, Zack Williams, Karie Kobe, and others. I noticed I wasn't so frustrated with the traffic or with people when I arrived at work or a store.

I noticed I was becoming a more thoughtful person and certainly was a lot more compassionate.

Are you able to memorize music verses easier than memorizing Bible verses?

I also started reading my Bible more, but not on a planned schedule, and certainly not an everyday morning devotion like I do now.

What I started to understand—although it took about six years of going to church every week and being involved in outreach programs—was that I really felt like Jesus was my true friend no matter what I did. No matter how many times I stumbled, Jesus is always there for me, and He wants to be your best friend too.

The song "Who Am I" makes me think. Who do I think I am, that Jesus would choose to show me the way to walk with Him even though my heart would wander away from Jesus and try to do things on my own? Certainly it is not because who I am, but because of Jesus's death on the cross and the resurrection, that I can be saved and live in heaven for eternity.

Nothing I have done, no works or good deeds, can get me into heaven. It is because God gives us grace and forgiveness that I have eternal life with my Father in heaven, and I will be reunited with my mom and dad, family members, and friends! Amen and hallelujah.

God hears every thought we have, every word we speak, and

every word spoken to us. Even when I sin, Jesus is right there to catch me and reminds me I am a child of the Most High God, perfectly made in His image, strong and brave. I know I belong to Him, my Savior, my Friend.

Do you need a friend in Jesus? Do you need a safety net to catch you when you sin? If you don't have a personal relationship with Jesus, you can start that relationship today. Just say, "Jesus, I am a sinner, and I'm asking You to forgive me of my sins. I believe in the Father, Son, and Holy Ghost, and I want to start a personal relationship with You, Jesus. Come into my heart. I want to walk out the rest of my life in accordance to Your will. Amen."

Congratulations! The angels throw a party in heaven every time a new believer comes home to their heavenly Father. Your family and friends in heaven are cheering you on!

Please contact me at i-Praise Internet Church (www.i-Praise.org) and leave me a comment, which goes directly into my email. I would love to pray for you and with you. We are here to try to answer your questions, and if we don't know the answer, we will find the answer and get back to you.

Get in a good Bible-based church that teaches and trains from the Bible and shows you how to have a personal relationship with your friend Jesus.

NOTES

Four

Christians Judging Others

One of the biggest reasons I left the church and God was because the "Christians" I knew and met were always judging people and me.

The Casting Crowns song "Jesus, Friend of Sinner" talks about Jesus being a friend of sinners like me and you. Even though we have moved away from Jesus, He still wants a close, personal relationship with us. Some Christians think it is our responsibility to cut down people, especially brothers and sister in Christ, but it is not our place to behave like that.

> Don't pick on people, jump on their failures, criticize their faults—unless, of course, you want the same treatment. That critical spirit has a way of boomeranging. It's easy to see a smudge on your neighbor's face and be oblivious to the ugly sneer on your own. Do you have the nerve to say, "Let me wash your face for you," when your own face is distorted by contempt? It's this whole traveling road-show mentality all over again, playing a holier-than-thou part instead of just living your part. Wipe that ugly sneer off your own face, and you might be

> fit to offer a washcloth to your neighbor. (Matthew 7:1–5 MSG)

Ouch!

Folks, you really need to get this scripture down deep in your soul because it is the number one reason why people don't choose to follow Jesus. We create people like me who run from the church and from God.

This scripture is part of Jesus's message called the Sermon on the Mount, and there were thousands of people listening to Jesus's teaching.

Have ever been judged by a Christian?

I heard Rick say the other day on his Sunday Message, "There are two reasons why someone does not become a Christian, (1) because they have never met a Christian, and (2) because they met a Christian." Boy, is that ever so true!

I like what Joel Osteen says about judging others: "Your job isn't to judge. Your job isn't to figure out if someone deserves something or decide who is right or wrong. Your job is to lift the fallen, restore the broken, and heal the hurting."(please visit www.goodreads.com/quotes/120352-your-job-is-not-to-judge)

In Pew Research Center telephone surveys conducted in 2018 and 2019, 65 percent of American adults describe themselves as Christians when asked about their religion, down 12 percentage points over the past decade. In that same study, people who describe their religious identity as atheist, agnostic, or "nothing in particular" now stand at 26 percent, up from 17 percent in 2009. (please visit www.pewforum.org/2019/10/17/in-u-s-decline)

In another Pew survey, they asked, "Why do people attend church?" Here are some of the most popular answers. (please visit www.pewforum.org/2018/08/01 why-Americans-go-to-religous-services)

- To become a better person (68%)
- To introduce faith to their kids (69%)

- To find personal comfort (66%)
- To grow closer to God (81%)

Another interesting fact that came out of this same study shows that 20 percent of adults attending services monthly or more say they don't feel any real connection to God during church. A surprising 40 percent don't feel a connection to their faith.

I truly believe this a huge problem for our churches and for the Christian community.

If 20 percent of adults attending church do not feel connected to God, their behaviors toward others will also be ungodly. When 40 percent of people going to church do not feel connected to their faith, then these same 40 percent are not going to be a strong example for nonbelievers or prodigals.

It does not take much for prodigal children to leave the church and God again because they are already apprehensive of Christians and the church's teachings. If there are 40 percent of the people attending church who do not feel connected to their faith, they will offend new believers and prodigals like myself.

This is why I tell everyone, "Don't blame God for what people do."

Do not depend on a church or the people in it to bring you closer to God. It is our responsibility to develop our own personal relationships with Jesus.

Once I figured that out, my life started to change for the better. Once I got the need for acceptance from church and other Christians out of my head, I had room to fill it with the love of Jesus.

I remember one time our church was having a chili cookoff, and I love to make chili, so I said I would enter. One of the pastors who was running the event told me they were not getting very many people to sign up and didn't know if there would be enough chili for the crowd they were expecting, so he asked if I would make three gallons of chili, and I said sure.

The night of the chili cookoff came, and people were bringing their crock pots of chili into the kitchen area where I had my three gallons of chili. I had spent close to two hundred dollars on the ingredients and two days preparing and cooking. Crock pots were everywhere, and they were trying to decide which chili they were going to put in the chaffing dishes for people to eat and vote.

There was enough chili to feed the masses and have plenty leftover for another chili cookoff.

I heard people saying, "We have to put this person's chili out because she is the wife of a longtime member of the church. Oh, we have to put this one out, or she will get really upset, and we don't want her upset!" On and on it went, but no one mentioned putting any of my three gallons out for people to eat and judge.

I had recently joined the church, and this was my first event so nobody knew me, and I did not know many people who were there.

My thoughts immediately went back to my mistreatment at the church I had left and the Christians I had tried to associate with when I was seventeen years old. I had the same feeling of, "If this is how Christians behave, I don't want to be associated with them—and if God is allowing it, I don't want Him either."

This was in 2015. I had been back following Jesus for almost twenty years, yet I still had these feeling inside.

You know it is Satan, right? He is telling us these things so we will walk away from Jesus and give our souls back to him.

Fortunately, my faith was much stronger, and I was so much more forgiving when this happened. I asked God for grace, and I forgave them for totally ignoring me.

I decided, "If they don't want to put out my chili, I will put it out myself!" For the next two hours, I brought out all my chili, and people said they really liked it. I did not win, but at least I gave with a joyous heart.

The next event was the yearly Halloween party, and our Bible study groups were asked to sign up for booths and games that we would set up and run. We all had the big red and blue buckets that people would normally place ice and drinks in at parties. Each game booth had one of these big buckets full of assorted candy.

The event was a community event, so there were many people there with their kids and grandkids, and many did not go to church or even know who Jesus is.

Our game had cups scattered around on a table, and the kids had ping-pong balls that they must toss into the cup, and the ball must stay inside to get a piece of candy. We were to add up the number of balls in the cups after thirty seconds, and that was the number of pieces we were to give the kids.

We are talking maybe ten cups, so the most candy they could win was ten pieces, but the average child won three to four pieces.

After about two hours into the three-hour event, we had not made a dent in the bucket of candy, so I decided to start giving two or three pieces per cup. Now the average kid was walking away with six to ten pieces of candy.

As the story spread about this guy giving away a lot of candy, our line started to grow, so I gave away more candy each time. The parents and kids were laughing and having a great time—until the "resident candy control officer" from the church came by to see what all the excitment was about at our game booth.

When she saw me handing out handfuls of candy to each kid, she told me to stop and stated I was no longer allowed to work at the game booth. She said, "We have rules, and if we expect the kids to follow them, we also expect the adults to follow them as well."

I said, "look at the bucket! We still have half of it left. I thought we were here to have fun with the kids and to show them the love of Jesus." I have since left that church—not for this reason, but it was a part of my decision and a big part of my memory regarding how we cannot let other people destroy our joy.

My faith has grown so much over the years, so I check myself when I see or hear fellow "Christians" saying or doing things that do not show the love of Jesus. I try very hard to show them God's grace.

This has been so liberating to me as a prodigal child. The attitudes of others that Satan used to irritate me and cause me to take it out on God, and even leave God, no longer affect my personal relationship with God or Jesus.

Would you like to have this same feeling of liberation in your life?

We all can find peace and joy in the words and actions of our personal Savior, Jesus Christ.

The song "Jesus, Friend of Sinners" is saying that Jesus is a friend to all of us sinners, and that includes everyone, no matter one's maturity as a Christian or whether one is not a Christian. It is saying that as the church, we must stop criticizing everyone who is not our same faith or doesn't believe or preach in the way we like. We must stop pointing fingers and start opening our hands to help others. It is time we, as the image of God, stop talking and start showing the love of Jesus to everyone.

> For We all sin and fall short of the Glory of God. (Romans 3:23 NIV)

There is a story in the Bible where Jesus was in a square by the temple, and the Pharisees brought him a woman caught in adultery. Of course nothing happens to the man, but they stoned to death any women caught in adultery.

> They were trying to trap him into saying something they could use against him, but Jesus stooped down and wrote in the dust with his finger. They kept demanding an answer, so he stood up again and said, "All right, but let the one who has never sinned throw the first stone!" Then he stooped down again and wrote in the dust. (John 8:6–8 NLT)

All the men dropped their stones and walked away. Jesus helped the women up.

> Then Jesus stood up again and said to the woman, "Where are your accusers? Didn't even one of them condemn you?" "No, Lord," she said. And Jesus said, "Neither do I. Go and sin no more." (John 8:10–11 NLT)

This lady sinned, and Jesus was there to show her His mercy and grace just like He shows us sinners that same mercy and grace.

The story reminds us of the mercy and grace of Jesus toward us when we do not deserve it, and we should drop to our knees in praise. People know only what we as Christian are against; they do not know what we are for. We need to get over the condemning and start showing the love of Jesus.

We Christian's have earned the reputation from non-Christians because we sometimes judge people, especially those who are really hurting and are looking for help, not condemnation. Christian's are trying to play God, and that turns people off to God.

What if we put down our signs (all the stuff we are against), crossed over the lines (getting in people's lives, no matter how messy), and showed the love of Jesus like I experienced at Saddleback Church? Had Saddleback Church not shown me Jesus love, and had Rick Warren not taught of acceptance and nonjudgment behavior, I believe I would have never restored my relationship with Jesus and never started my walk to my purpose on Earth.

This is one of my biggest pet peeves with Christians: judging other people.

We will never get nonbelievers to listen and accept Jesus as their Savior when we, who are sinners ourselves, are judging their sins but do not expect anyone to judge our own sins.

That is why I started i-Praise Internet Church, and you can look it up at www.i-Praise.org. So many people I met did not like to go to brick-and-mortar church or didn't have time due to work or the kids' weekend activities.

There are several messages from me on the website, and I

encourage you to listen to them. I speak about showing the love of Jesus to people from any walk of life and from any place they are at in their lives.

As followers of Jesus, we need to be like Jesus Christ and show our love to the "lost cause" and the outcasts.

Jesus is our living example to love the unlovable.

I thought, "What perfect words for me to remember." Before I started my new relationship with Jesus, I was a lost cause and an outcast. Then Jesus came into my life, and He forgave me and forgot all my sins. Now I can have a close, personal relationship with Him.

Is it time for you to stop running away from Jesus and return home as a prodigal child, like me?

NOTES

Five

Tired of Fighting the Daily Battle

There is a song by Michael W. Smith "Surrounded," (Fight My Battles). The words remind me of the story of Elisha.
In 2 Kings 6:8–23 (NIV), the Bible says,

> Now the king of Aram was at war with Israel. After conferring with his officers, he said, "I will set up my camp in such and such a place."
>
> The man of God sent word to the king of Israel: "Beware of passing that place, because the Arameans are going down there." So the king of Israel checked on the place indicated by the man of God. Time and again Elisha warned the king, so that he was on his guard in such places.
>
> This enraged the king of Aram. He summoned his officers and demanded of them, "Tell me! Which of us is on the side of the king of Israel?"

"None of us, my lord the king," said one of his officers, "but Elisha, the prophet who is in Israel, tells the king of Israel the very words you speak in your bedroom."

"Go, find out where he is," the king ordered, "so I can send men and capture him." The report came back: "He is in Dothan." Then he sent horses and chariots and a strong force there. They went by night and surrounded the city."

When the servant of the man of God got up and went out early the next morning, an army with horses and chariots had surrounded the city. "Oh no, my lord! What shall we do?" the servant asked."

"Don't be afraid," the prophet answered. "Those who are with us are more than those who are with them."

And Elisha prayed, "Open his eyes, LORD, so that he may see." Then the LORD opened the servant's eyes, and he looked and saw the hills full of horses and chariots of fire all around Elisha.

As the enemy came down toward him, Elisha prayed to the LORD, "Strike this army with blindness." So he struck them with blindness, as Elisha had asked.

Elisha told them, "This is not the road and this is not the city. Follow me, and I will lead you to the man you are looking for." And he led them to Samaria.

> After they entered the city, Elisha said, "Lord, open the eyes of these men so they can see." Then the Lord opened their eyes and they looked, and there they were, inside Samaria.
>
> When the king of Israel saw them, he asked Elisha, "Shall I kill them, my father? Shall I kill them?"
>
> "Do not kill them," he answered. "Would you kill those you have captured with your own sword or bow? Set food and water before them so that they may eat and drink and then go back to their master." So, he prepared a great feast for them, and after they had finished eating and drinking, he sent them away, and they returned to their master. The bands from Aram stopped raiding Israel's territory.

Do you feel like I do sometimes, when I get up in the morning and think, "I must get ready for another battle today"?

I am sure Elisha felt like he did not want a battle that day. He did not plan any defensive moves to protect himself or the city. But Elisha knew that his God was mightier than any army of soldiers. Now his servant needed to be encouraged and see firsthand what Elisha knew in his heart and mind. Elisha prayed for God to open the eyes of his servant so he could see the power of the angelic army of God surrounding the king's army.

Then Elisha prayed to God to blind all the soldiers so they could not see whom they were talking to, and he led them blindly to the Israeli army, where they were captured without a single injury on either side.

When Elisha was asked about the punishment of the prisoners, Elisha showed the mercy of God to them, fed them, and sent them back home. Because he did not harm them and treated them respectfully, the king of Aram never attacked the Israelites again, saving thousands of lives on both sides.

Does anybody reading this book feel like I did most of my life, fighting daily battles? Every day there seems to be another battle to face, or they are already going on from the day before.

From this scripture, God wants us to know that no matter the odds against us, God's angelic army is surrounding whatever worldly army is against us. We might not see them, like the servant, because he was looking through his worldly eyes. But if we look at our battles through the eyes and words from God, like Elisha did, we can rest in His promises of peace, love, joy, compassion, and comfort.

Are you a parent or an employer, and the people around you need you to be strong even when you do not feel strong at all?

I am both a parent and employer, and I cannot express how much pressure our kids and our employees place on us. It is not because they are being mean, at least most of the time!

I know when we were raising our kids, somedays I wanted to say, "Stop! I don't want to have to make all these decisions today. Somebody step up—I'm tired. Go away."

If you are like me and own your own business, you have employees to worry about. Do we have enough sales this week to make payroll? What if business slows down? Let's grab the Jesus genie off the shelf and start rubbing … "Oh, Jesus, help me make payroll, Jesus. If you help me make payroll and give me the money to pay my bills, then I will start tithing at my home church. I am going to finally start saving 10 percent of my income—just send me the money I need. Thank You, Jesus."

But Jesus is not a genie for us to pull off the shelf when we get in trouble. We need to be walking in step with Jesus every day, talking to Him, praising Him, thanking Him, reading the Bible, and studying His teachings. Take the time to show others the love of Jesus through your good works and deeds. Then when you need Jesus because you are low on your cash flow, it is already part of your normal daily relationship with Jesus.

A week or so later, a sale comes in that you were working on for a couple of months, and you have the money you need to make payroll, pay your bills, and have some money leftover. Then you think, "Boy, I'm glad I finally closed that sale," not "Thank You, God, for the sale I was working on so hard." This is not being a true follower of God! I am sorry if I offend someone, but we do not need Sunday Christians to fight our battles. We need prayer warriors and evangelists. We need disciples making more disciples.

Jesus was there for the last sale, and the one before that, and the one after this one. Jesus is not a genie.

If we have a personal relationship with Jesus, He is with us always. We must stop thinking that we are in control until things get out of control, and then we can grab the Jesus genie bottle and rub away.

Some days I do not even feel like getting out of bed, but God reminds me every day that I have responsibilities to my family, my employees, and their families. So I first thank God that I am awake, I am breathing, I can see, I can hear, I can move, and I can get up out of bed most days pain free. Millions of other people would love to have these blessing on their lives.

My prodigal brothers and sisters reading this book, stay strong. Listen to what God says, not people; only God and Jesus have our answers. Abide in His Word and walk with Jesus hand in hand on the earth.

> I know what I'm doing. I have it all planned out—plans to take care of you, not abandon you, plans to give you the future you hope for. When you call on me, when you come and pray to me, I'll listen. When you come looking for me, you'll find me. (Jerimiah 29:11–13 MSG)

Jeremiah was a prophet and the son of Hilkiah, who was a Jewish priest. He was born in 650 BC and died in 570 BC, so he was about eighty years old when he died. He came from the Benjamite village of Anathoth.

He is writing to the captive people in Babylon, telling them to stop worrying. I feel these words are saying to me that God sees and knows these problems, and He is handling them even if we cannot see what God is doing (like Elisha's servant).

Most of the time when Christians get in trouble or life throws us a curveball, we first try to handle them ourselves. A sudden death of a loved one, a loss of a job, a child out of control. Maybe the housing market dropped, and you find yourself losing your home. We grab our Jesus genie bottle and start rubbing away. Then we find out Jesus is not a genie. We start praying, Lord Jesus, please take this problem from me right now. I cannot take this anymore, and You said for us to call on You, and You will answer my pray. Well, Father, You have an hour to take care of it!" No, Jesus is not a genie, so you cannot simply grab Jesus off the shelf whenever you need something and expect Him to come out of the bottle, and poof—all problems are gone.

Now, God could do that if He wanted to, because He's God. But I can tell you from my years back walking with the Lord and having a very deep and personal relationship with God and Jesus that He doesn't work that way in my life.

Jeremiah is being challenged by false prophets, and he is telling the captives to stay strong and believe. This is God speaking through His prophet in Jeremiah 29:11 (MSG).

> I know what I'm doing. I have it all planned out—
> plans to take care of you, not abandon you, plans
> to give you the future you hope for.

The Bible teaches us to not worry about that lost job; that did not surprise God, but He knows what He is doing. Let us walk with Him, talk to Him, and place our burden on Him, and we will see His miracle for a better job. We are running through the maze of life, but we can have a clear picture of our path when we have Jesus looking down on His children from heaven, giving us safe directions.

Have you ever seen a hedge maze? The hedge is eight to ten feet tall, and you have a series of open areas between the tall hedge, without being able to see the entire hedge maze. The object is that you walk into the opening on one end. You follow the open path in front of you, walking straight or turning left or right, until you hit a dead-end. Then you backtrack to where you were and turn the other way to see where that leads you. You continue to do this until you finally reach the opening at the other end of the maze. You walk out into the open and can see all around you. It can take you hours to get through the maze depending how big it is, but at some point, you finally make it through. Let us say it took one hour for you to figure it out.

Let me ask you a question. What if you had a coach, a guide, or a partner hovering in a helicopter one hundred feet up, and that person was looking down at you in the maze?

You have your cell phone on and ear buds in, and your coach is telling you how to get through the maze. The person can see all the safe places to walk and the obstacles in your way. Your person can guide you, coach you, and walk you through the maze quicker and more safely than you could on your own.

Do you feel that you are in a maze and cannot find your way out, or your way back?

Jesus is our helicopter pilot hovering above our lives, guiding us safely through the maze of life, and showing us when to move forward and which turns to make with each obstacle we encounter. By following His Word, we can navigate life in peace, in comfort, and in joy.

> Trust in the LORD with all your heart and lean not on your own understanding; in all your ways submit to him, and he will make your paths straight. (Proverbs 3:5 NIV)

I really like what the Message translation in the Bible says in Proverbs 3:5–12.

> Trust God from the bottom of your heart; don't try to figure out everything on your own.
>
> Listen for God's voice in everything you do, everywhere you go; he's the one who will keep you on track.
>
> Don't assume that you know it all. Run to God! Run from evil!
>
> Your body will glow with health, your very bones will vibrate with life!
>
> Honor God with everything you own; give him the first and the best. Your barns will burst, your wine vats will brim over.
>
> But don't, dear friend, resent God's discipline; don't sulk under his loving correction.
>
> It's the child he loves that God corrects; a father's delight is behind all this.

Do yourselves a big favor and do not read only one translation of the Bible. I read the New International Version, The Message, the New King James Version, and the Living Bible translations when I am reading scripture and preparing my weekly message for i-Praise Internet Church, which I started on Easter Sunday 2019.

We started with five followers of that first day, and now we have over 1,500 followers whom we get the pleasure to minister to several times a day.

Thank You, Lord Jesus, for the blessings You have given us to serve Your children and show them the love of Jesus in a real and meaningful way, through i-Praise.org. Father, We are reaching prodigals like myself, bringing Your sheep back into Your fold. In Jesus's name, amen.

I have also learned that when you feel blessings from the Lord, you need to stop immediately so you do not miss the blessing. Then thank Him and praise His name. We receive the blessing back from God when we thank Him. I do not know about you, but I want to make sure I am in line to receive as many blessings as God has stored up for me.

I know that when I left the church and pushed Jesus out of my life at seventeen years old, I tried to run through my maze of life by myself. For twenty years, I constantly ran into obstacles, roadblocks, pain, fear, and frustration, trying to just get through a small part of the maze myself each day. I tried to navigate the maze myself, and it was not until I surrendered my life to Jesus again after all the mistakes, all the destruction I had created in my life and others around me. I felt like Jesus has me in the palm of His hands. Jesus is holding my hand, and I am walking you through the maze so I can find the comfort and the peace I am looking for. He will light our path, and He will hover above us, guiding us and protecting us.

Let us look at what God is telling us in this passage.

Trust God from the bottom of your heart, don't try to figure out everything on your own. (Proverbs 3:5 MSG)It does not say, "Trust God on the surface of our hearts." It says we must trust God from the bottom of our hearts. That mean deep down in our hearts. This is not suggested as a surface trust. No, this is a deep trust because it comes from the bottom of our hearts.

Down at the bottom of our hearts is where the good stuff is. That is the same place we find that super deep love of our spouses, our kids, and our close friends. This is not the same level when we say to a coworker or a friendly acquaintance, "I love the way you do your job. I love the outfit you are wearing today." Surface love is the top of the heart love.

But I say to you, "Trust God from the bottom of your heart."

It goes on the say, "Don't try to figure it out on your own." God has already written you His manual for a happy life, called the Bible. Read it, study it, and abide in it, and when it gets deep inside your heart, trust it.

Our God can look down at our lives and guide us through the hedge maze of life. The Lord and His Word help us turn left, or we will run into a drug dealer. Jesus wants to protect us. He may say, "Turn right here, or you are going be make a bad financial decision." Jesus can see from up above. We might need to make an immediate right turn because Satan is sending his troops into the maze to mess us up so we will stop listening to Jesus and follow the world. If we walk straight, Jesus will lead us safely out of the maze of life.

One of my favorite Bible verses is Philippians 4:6–7 (ESV).

> Do not be anxious about anything, but in everything by prayer and supplication with thanksgiving let your requests be made known to God. And the peace of God, which surpasses all understanding, will guard your hearts and your minds in Christ Jesus.

This scripture was written by Paul around AD 62, and over two thousand years later, God's Word is saying the same thing today.

Another translation of Philippians 4:6 comes from the Contemporary English Version (CEV).

> Don't worry about anything, but pray about everything. With thankful hearts offer up your prayers and requests to God.

The great thing about the Bible is God is saying the same thing over two thousand year ago, and those same truths are relevant today.

Before I recommitted my life back to God and Jesus and was baptized, I cannot tell you how many times I had been be on my knees and crying out to God, to Jesus, to get me through the night or the next day, but Jesus seemed so far away. I could not feel Him close. But God's inspired Word is saying to you and me that we are not alone.

Do you ever feel like you are grabbing for help, for hope, and you need God to guide your steps through your maze of life?

Sometimes we want something so badly that we grab at whatever we think will make us feel better. We are grabbing onto drugs and alcohol to kill the pain, even though we all realize it is just a temporary painkiller. We grab onto bad relationships because we feel these people are the only ones who will love us because they are like us. But what we are doing is not good for us, and by grabbing onto a person doing the same things, it is not good for either of us.

We cannot really be at rest when we are doing the holding. To truly rest, to totally relax the way Jesus wants us to rest, He wants us "to just be held" by Him. *Jesus answered them in John 16:31–35 (MSG).*

> Do you finally believe? In fact, you're about to make a run for it—saving your own skins and abandoning me. But I'm not abandoned. The Father is with me. I've told you all this so that trusting me, you will be unshakable and assured, deeply at peace. In this godless world you will continue to experience difficulties. But take heart! I've conquered the world.

These verses are saying to me, "Hey, folks, do you finally get it? Do you finally believe what Jesus is teaching us and is walking it out for us?" You might run and try abandoning God, but I never feel abandoned or alone because my Father, God, is always with me. He told us this truth, and Jesus has modeled this truth for us. When we finally get it out of our heads that we are the masters of our own destiny and start trusting God, we will be "unshakable and assured, deeply at peace."

Has anyone noticed how much more godless our country is over the past ten to twenty years? Maybe it is because I am a prodigal, and I am always a little uncomfortable pointing out observations because I do not want to act judgmental to others like Christians were to me. Please take this observation with an open heart. Does it seem to you that our fellow Christian brothers and sisters are now more godless in their walk with the Lord than in the past?

We miss church one week because one of the kids has a Sunday game that starts at noon, and it is two hours away. We could have gone Saturday night, but that's not the regular group we like to hang out with, so God will understand and will show us His mercy and grace. He will shower us with His blessing because that is who God is.

Then the morning comes, and we have hit the snooze button three times, so we jump out of the bed and go right into the shower. We are now in hurry mode as we start getting ready to go to work, or get the kids ready, or do whatever daily routines in our house. We missed reading our Bible verses for the day, and we missed our quiet time thanking God for the breath He gave us, the sight He gave us, the health He gave us, the job He gave us, and the kids He gave us. God gives it all to us every day we are alive, but do we give back to Him by spending time with Him, praying and connecting to Him? Do we give God the time and respect He deserves each day by reading and being taught His love letters, His Word, the Bible?

I see our country and our world being more godless in a time when we need more God. Several Bible scholars and pastors say we are in the end-time, the Second Coming of Jesus. They say that there are many things happening in our country and in our world that are fulfilling the prophecy in the Book of Revelations.

I have never been to seminary college, and my father and grandfathers were not pastors or Bible teachers, so Revelations confuses me. I will lean on those people to discuss the topic in detail or specifics. We all need to get into a good Bible study on Revelations. I suggest going to Jerry Dirmann's YouTube channel and looking for his chapter-by-chapter teaching on the Book of Revelations.

This is what the Moody Institute says about the Second Coming of Christ. (please see www.moodybible.org/beliefs/positional-statements/second-coming)

> Before He establishes His kingdom on earth, Jesus will come for His Church, an event commonly referred to as the "Rapture."
>
> At that time, the dead in Christ will be raised and living Christians will be caught up to meet the Lord in the air and be with Him forever.
>
> After the Rapture of the Church, Christians will be brought before the judgment seat of Christ. He will reward them on the basis of the works they have accomplished. This is not a judgment to determine their salvation but a reward for their labor on Christ's behalf.

My prodigal brothers and sisters, we need to get this message deep in our hearts and souls. If we say that we believe in the Bible and that it is God's Word, we must believe 100 percent of the Bible. We do not get to pick and choose what scripture is for us and what parts do not apply. No, it is all or nothing! We must believe deep down in our hearts and not on the surface of our hearts.

When we are tired of fighting the battle of life, running through the maze of life, and not seeing our way clearly, we must finally surrender to the God, who placed us in our mothers' wombs, who breathed His life into us. We must stop holding on and should simply be held!

NOTES

Six

God Relentlessly Pursued Me

There is a song by Casting Crowns called "God of All My Days." The song says to me that I came to God when my heart was in pieces, broken by the world we live in, where Satan is the "god of the Earth."

What I found in my search for God was a God with the healing power to mend my broken heart and make all things new again.

The song goes on to say to me that when I have questions—because it can get so confusing being a Christian—God has all the answers and is full of wisdom. When I put my trust in God, He will take my hand and walk me through the storms of life.

There is a parable in the Book of Luke about a good shepherd who was tending his flock of one hundred sheep. Soon he realizes that one of the sheep is missing, so he leaves the ninety-nine to find his one sheep. His one lost sheep is more valuable than the ninety-nine safe sheep that remain. It is another parable of the prodigal story Jesus wants us to understand. Jesus is more interested in bringing the prodigals back into the Body of Christ so we can glorify the name of Jesus as His disciples and fulfill His purpose for our lives. Check out this parable of the lost sheep in Luke 15:1–7 (NIV).

> Now the tax collectors and sinners were all gathering around to hear Jesus. But the Pharisees and the teachers of the law muttered, "This man welcomes sinners and eats with them."
>
> Then Jesus told them this parable: "Suppose one of you has a hundred sheep and loses one of them. Doesn't he leave the ninety-nine in the open country and go after the lost sheep until he finds it? And when he finds it, he joyfully puts it on his shoulders and goes home. Then he calls his friends and neighbors together and says, 'Rejoice with me; I have found my lost sheep.' I tell you that in the same way there will be more rejoicing in heaven over one sinner who repents than over ninety-nine righteous persons who do not need to repent."

For me as a prodigal who was hurt by the people and leadership of the church, I was leery about going back to church or starting a relationship with Jesus. I knew my life was a mess! Jesus and the church had become so foreign to me that it took a suggestion from a close friend to try Saddleback Church in 1995.

I remembered how, when I read in the Bible about the love and compassion of Jesus, it made my heart feel good and gave me comfort. I believe that was God relentlessly pursuing me even after all that I had done in my life.

The words to this song sounded like me talking to God. Every day I started praying more often, and now I pray many, many times each day because I want to feel God's presence in me and around me.

I have said it before, and I will continue to say it throughout this book: Rick Warren was the first person, and Saddleback Church was the first church, that helped me see Jesus in the flesh. What I read about in the Bible about Jesus and His Father, God, was what I saw being taught at Saddleback. The love of Jesus was what I saw being walked out with Rick, Kay, and the rest of the Saddleback team. The people attending and serving at the church were friendly, ready to help answer questions, and ready to make me feel at home like Jesus.

I believed in my heart that if God and Jesus were really pursuing me like Rick was teaching, then I wanted to have a relationship with God and Jesus and see where it took me.

I was in a really bad marriage at the time and the thought of having a "relationship" with anyone seemed scary, but the thought of not taking a chance with God and Jesus seemed even scarier. So, I surrendered my life again to Jesus in 1996 and was Baptized at Saddleback Church in 2006.

> Take Up the Cross and Follow Him. Then Jesus said to His disciples, "If anyone desires to come after Me, let him deny himself, and take up his cross, and follow Me. For whoever desires to save his life will lose it, but whoever loses his life for My sake will find it." (Matthew 16:24–25 NKJV)

Although I knew God was pursuing me, I also needed to be pursuing Him and His teachings. This verse in the Book of Matthew shows Jesus talking and teaching His disciples: "If anyone comes after me, they must first deny himself."

We must first say, "I cannot do this on my own. I am not wise enough, strong enough, or talented enough, so I am going to take up the cross." We must reestablish our salvation as prodigals through the cross and the resurrection and start following God and Jesus.

Then it says in Matthew 16:25 (NIV),

> For whoever wishes to save his life will lose it; but whoever loses his life for My sake will find it.

Jesus is warning us here, and we need to pay close attention to what Jesus is saying.

If we think we can save our own lives, living under our own power and our own will, Jesus is showing us and teaching us through His Word, the Bible, that we will be lost living like this, and we will die and go to Hades.

Praise God and His glory! Thank You, Jesus, for bringing us life after death! Amen!

My whole life is something that I had to finally surrender to God, and my life has never been the same since.

Have you ever heard about to story of Jesus telling the disciples that He was going to stay behind and pray after feeding five thousand men, plus women and children, with seven loaves of bread and two fish? Jesus wanted them to take one of the fishing boats to the other side of the Sea of Galilee, and He would meet them at the other side of the lake after Jesus rested and prayed. The disciples launch the fishing boat out into the sea, but after they were quite a way from the shore, the winds start coming in, the sail flapped, and the boat was tossed from side to side and up and down as the waves swelled. The disciples were afraid. Off in the distance, a disciple saw a figure coming toward them. They thought at first it was a ghost. But then my hero, Peter, thought he recognized it might be Jesus. Peter was fighting off the wind and seawater blowing into his eyes. They were now in a full-blown storm.

> "Lord, if it's you," Peter replied, "tell me to come to you on the water."
>
> "Come," he [Jesus] said. Then Peter got down out of the boat, walked on the water and came toward Jesus. But when he saw the wind, he was afraid and, beginning to sink, cried out, "Lord, save me!"
>
> Immediately Jesus reached out his hand and caught him. "You of little faith," he said, "why did you doubt?" And when they climbed into the boat, the

> wind died down. Then those who were in the boat worshiped him, saying, "Truly you are the Son of God." (Matthew 14:28–33 NIV)

I think this is a good illustration for me because we see Jesus walking or pursuing the disciples in the boat, and Peter was pursing Jesus on the water.

The disciples were in this fishing boat with the sail up, going to the other side to meet up with Jesus. I am sure Jesus already knew what was going to happen—He was God in the flesh, after all. But Jesus was giving His disciples an opportunity to also pursue Him by showing their faith!

Peter was bold, brash, foul-mouthed, and a typical "man of the sea." He saw someone in the distance walking toward them. Peter finally recognized the person to be Jesus, so Peter stepped out of the boat in the middle of the storm and started walking on the water toward Jesus, because Peter's faith was so strong at that moment.

The same thing happens to so many Christians. We start out having a strong faith in Jesus, and all is going well. Then the storms of life rise up. Next thing we know, our faith is shattered, and we start sinking and drowning in sin. But if we keep our faith in Jesus, even when we stumble, we can reach out our hands, and He will walk us through the storm and to safe, dry ground.

Jesus loves to see our faith rise up, and through our faith, the Bible says that we can do all the things that our hearts desire.

Jesus saw that faith in Peter, and He simply said, "Come." Peter stepped out of the boat and onto the water.

When we fix our eyes on Jesus and surrender our own will, the Bible says in Philippians 4:13 (NKJV), "I can do all things through Christ Jesus who strengthens me." Right?

Peter was fine walking on the water because his eyes were fixed on Jesus, but like all our lives, he turned from Jesus even when he knew better. We have seen miracles in our lives and in others, just as Peter and the disciples saw. They had just witnessed Jesus taking a few loaves of bread and a few fish to feed five thousand men; we know there were also women and children there, but in those days, men were the "important ones" in that culture, so they were the ones who were counted.

Now, Peter knew the power of God through Jesus, but like us, it did not take much to distract him. The wind distracted Peter. As soon as Peter took his eyes off Jesus and looked at a potential problem, the wind, he immediately lost his faith and started to sink!

Have you ever been in a storm in your life? You have your eyes fixed on Jesus, and you are starting to feel victory—but then something distracts you, and you feel you are sinking again.

What happened to Peter when he felt himself sinking?

> But when he saw the wind, he was afraid, and beginning to sink he cried out, "Lord, save me." Jesus immediately reached out his hand and took hold of him, saying to him, "O you of little faith, why did you doubt?" (Matthew 14:30–31 ESV)

Jesus used this as a teachable moment for Peter and the rest of the disciples watching. The Bible says, "Immediately Jesus reached out His hand and caught him." But then the teaching moment happened, and Jesus said to Peter, "You of little faith, why did you doubt?"

I can just image what most of us think. "Too bad, Peter. You said you had faith, and Jesus showed you what you could do with your life, but your lack of faith blew it for you, so if you drown, it's your own fault."

We have in us the same power as our Father, but like Peter, with one distraction, we take our focus off Jesus. That distraction becomes our new god. Our eyes are focused on a potential problem, and that will cause our lives to sink.

But instead, the Bible teaches us in Matthew 14:31 (NIV), "Immediately Jesus reached out his hand and caught him."

Prodigal brothers and sisters, nonbelievers, and all levels of mature Christians, focus on the word *immediately*. What does that mean? It means to me that before anything else can happen, this event must happen first—immediately. Not sometime soon, when it is convenient, or when we get around to it. No, this is right now, this microsecond, immediately. Peter blew it and lost his faith at that moment, but his savior immediately reached out His hand and brought this "lost soul" back to the boat, or back to the flock as we read earlier.

Are you distracted from God's Word and your relationship with Jesus?

Jesus will immediately reach out His hand, get you back in the boat, calm the seas and the winds, and bring you safely out of the storm and back onto solid ground.

The Casting Crowns song "God of All My Days" states, "Even though I ran from you as a prodigal and ended up in dark places, and no matter where or what I am doing wrong, God relentlessly pursues me and you." I was embarrassed by my failures, like the young prodigal who left home and returned. Like him, I finally fell into my heavenly Father's arms and asked for His mercy and grace. As I prayed more, worshipped more, and stayed connected in God's Word, God gave me His grace that always covers me.

What are you running from? Because we all are running from something.

This was me! I ran from God and the church because I allowed distractions—in this case, people—to take my eyes off God and Jesus. I found myself wandering in the shadows and in the bars, drinking and misbehaving. I tried to hide from Jesus because I felt so unworthy to be called His son and to be loved. I had turned my back on Him.

But what I learned at Saddleback is no matter how off far course I was, God's grace still covers me, and I am forgiven. Praise God! Thank You, Lord!

> In him we have redemption through his blood, the forgiveness of sins, in accordance with the riches of God's grace. (Ephesians 1:7 NIV)

Jesus gave His life in exchange for us so we could live for eternity with Him and His Father, God, in heaven.

If you are in a storm in your life right now and need to place your life in someone's hand, reach out of the boat and ask Jesus to grab it. I can promise you, without a doubt in my mind, that Jesus will immediately reach out with no hesitation, grab it, and lead you to safe ground.

Maybe you are a prodigal like me and have moved away from a personal relationship with Jesus, but you find yourself hiding from Jesus like I did, ashamed of your lifestyle and the way you treated people, especially Christians. You need Jesus leading your life, being under His power and not your own. You can correct that direction and turn your eyes to Jesus right now.

Say right now, "Lord Jesus, forgive me of my sins. I believe in the Father, the Son, and the Holy Spirit. Come into my life, and I will follow You until the day I die. I want to make You my Lord and Savior. Amen."

By saying that simple prayer, you have been born again into the family of God. From here to eternity, any sins you commit or have committed will be forgiven as long as you ask for forgiveness and turn away from that sin. Then you will spend eternity with your loved ones.

Please send me an email to let me know you made this important decision so I can answer any questions you might have or direct you to the right resources to get you the answers.

Start following me at www.i-Praise.org, and you can listen to my messages about the love of Jesus. We can also help you find a local church for you to get connected with.

You can also follow us with our new nonprofit ministry, All Lives Matter 2 God. Visit www.AllLivesMatter2God.org to find a ministry you might be interested in supporting.

NOTES

Seven

My Ministry Begins

The song "Here I Am, Lord" by Eric Tom, has a line that says, "Here I am, Lord. Is it I, Lord?"

It was in August 2010, about fourteen years after recommitting my life back to Jesus and promising to follow Him the rest of my life, that I had a dream that would change the direction of my life forever.

I thought I was I going to continue with my business until I retired, but God had other plans for me. I did not tell anyone about my dream for a few years. I wanted to pray over the dream and ask God for clarity before moving forward or certainly telling anyone.

After a few years of prayer, reading and studying my daily devotions, and listening to several messages at our church, messages from Joel Osteen, Greg Laurie, and Rick Warren, I felt the dream was real. I needed to do my part and start moving forward as God had instructed me.

You see, God had showed me in my dream that my purpose here on earth was to spread the great news of Jesus and His salvation to everyone I could reach. I would share my journey back to Jesus and God through a website, social media, writing a book, and public speaking. I would start a community nonprofit, and the money I raised was to be given to support rescue missions and other community nonprofits across the United States.

I saw myself sitting down at a desk and writing my book. I saw a vision of me speaking on a stage, sharing Jesus's love for us, and instructing how we can form strong, personal relationships with Him and with God. I saw our website and our Facebook page, and I could see myself working on my computer, adding material and sending out messages. I saw myself preparing written messages and verbal messages that I would record and send out.

Now, if you ever saw my grades in school regarding English or any subject that has to do with writing, you would know that I would not be capable or even interested in writing a book. This book is a miracle of God.

I had designed websites for my company and other clients, so that did not seem so far off base. I loved public speaking, so that also was not too far-fetched. But writing a book? No way! That must be the hand of God.

My parents were great role models for me on my journey back to Jesus and God. They had been followers of Jesus since they were in grade school and followed Him throughout their lives.

From what I remember, when we lived in Subic Bay, Philippines, during the Vietnam War from 1966 to 1968, my dad would go with his team to Vietnam about every three months and stay for three months. They would train when they were back at Subic Bay for three months.

My mom, Betty, would take my sister and me to the Ship's Servicemen Center when our dad was away, which was located right outside the main gate before the sailors would walk into the town where all the bars and prostitutes were waiting for them.

Inside the center, they had a pool table, a ping-pong table, and all kinds of board games like chess, checkers, Monopoly, and Chutes and Ladders, to name a few. We would sit with the sailors, talk to them, and play games with them. I am sure they had food and drinks for them to enjoy instead of them going into the sin-filled city of Olongapo.

When my dad was home, we would go to the center and go out

to minister to the Filipino people and the indigenous tribe's people around the island of Luzon. My sister and I would play with the kids and learn more about them.

As a young eleven- to thirteen-year-old male, my eyes were opened to the most amazing sites and God's wonder throughout our trips to the jungles or conferences in Manila or Baggio. I loved and still love the Philippines and the Filipino people. The country and the people have such a special part in my heart. I even joined the navy in hopes I would be able to go back and see the changes in the country and the people.

I injured my knee in bootcamp, and the navy did not want to take on the responsibility of me potentially becoming a hazard if I were on a ship and my knee gave out. If I could not climb up the metal ladders they have between decks, I could cause other sailors to be unable to get by me, and they could get hurt. They gave me an honorable medical discharge, and my hope to return to the Philippines seemed like it was over.

I think God knew my love for the country and the people, and in 2015 I went back to the Philippines as part of my consulting business. God is so amazing that He gave me my dream to return to the Philippines. As the Bible says in Psalm 37:3–4 (NIV),

> Trust in the Lord and do good; dwell in the land
> and enjoy safe pasture. Take delight in the Lord,
> and he will give you the desires of your heart.

I had recommitted my life back to Jesus and to God in 1996, and it was nineteen years until my prayer was answered. Another miracle!

How long have you been waiting for a prayer to be answered?

When I was in the Philippines on business, I had a chance to take one day off with my driver to explore Subic Bay. We found the elementary school I went to, the house we lived in on the base, and the apartments we lived in off base in Olongapo for seven months while waiting to move into base housing. It was such an awesome experience, and it was everything I hoped it would be. All the bars were gone because the navy gave the Philippine government the base to use as an international free trade zone. Many major US corporations had factories and offices on the base, but many sites had not changed in forty-seven years.

While driving through Olongapo, we saw the poor kids running around with just T-shirts on and no underwear. Elderly men and women sat by the sides of the roads resting, eating whatever they might find that day to eat, and cleaning themselves, their animals, and laundry in the same muddy river or stream.

The Filipino people love the Lord, and when they have a chance to praise Jesus, they do it with all their hearts, souls, and minds. Yet to me, it seemed like God was not there. The living conditions did not look any different, except the bars were gone because the Navy had left.

I realized that I was seeing the people through my eyes and not through God's eyes.

The Apostle Paul writes to his "up and coming" disciple Timothy in 1 Timothy 6:6–12 (NKJV),

> Now godliness with contentment is great gain. For we brought nothing into this world, and it is certain we can carry nothing out. And having food and clothing, with these we shall be content. But those who desire to be rich fall into temptation and a snare, and into many foolish and harmful lusts which drown men in destruction and perdition. For the love of money is a root of all kinds of evil, for which some have strayed from the faith in their greediness and pierced themselves through with many sorrows.

These people have no money, so they do not fall into all the traps and pain that money can cause people when misused. There is no greed, no envy, no waste, and no temptations that money can bring because they have no money!

I tell you this story because it has also changed how I look at material things now and how I try to serve the Lord. I have learned to be content where I am, to be satisfied that as long as I have shelter, food, and clothes, I have all God promised me.

Remember the words of the song: "Here I am, Lord. Is it I, Lord?" The rest of the song talks about us following Jesus wherever He leads us, calling out to us during the night and the promise we need to accept from Jesus that we will take care of His children.

This is what my parents said when they retired: "Here I am, Lord. Is it I, Lord?"

My parents were members of the United Methodist Church in Phoenix, Arizona, and they were part of a group called the Nomads. The Nomads were of group of about two hundred volunteers who traveled in their own fifth wheels and motorhomes around the United States providing handyman services to the Methodist churches, Boys and Girl camps, drug rehab facilities, and other organizations supported by the United Methodist Church. Talk about showing the love of God and Jesus! My dad was a handyman all his adult life. There was nothing my dad and a few of his friends could not repair or build.

These acts of kindness touched my heart and soul, and whenever they were in Southern California working, I would try to see them on the weekend. My mom and dad would show me around the project, and I would meet the other Nomads working with them.

This was a great foundation for my ministry because of what I saw in my dream about using the income from my ministry to support rescue missions and community outreaches. I could see firsthand how that money could be used to help so many people in need. I believe it was God giving me a physical vision of my purpose.

The song "Here I Am, Lord" is a song my parents and the Nomads would sing each day after their morning devotions. This is what we all should be saying: "Here I am, Lord. Is it I Lord?" because

God has a purpose for each and every one of us. He placed it in us when He breathed His life into us in our mothers' womb.

I remember the first time I saw Billy Graham with my parents and church youth group in 1963, at the Los Angeles Memorial Coliseum. The church chartered buses, and we went to see this evangelists who was drawing huge crowds. The *Los Angeles Times* article said, "On the last afternoon of the three-week revival, 134,254 people crowded in to hear Graham's sermon, the largest crowd ever assembled at that venue." Now, the seating capacity of the LA Coliseum is 78,467! There were almost double the capacity of the stadium that night to hear a message about salvation and the love of Jesus. (please see www.latimes.com/opinion/op-ed/LA-Oe-young-Billy-Graham-Los Angeles)

I guess I had suppressed how I felt that night when I saw Billy Graham on stage and all those people listening to his every word, because something inside me got so excited that night. Something inside me jumped with excitement, and I had a vision of me standing up there speaking.

In November 2004, I saw Billy Graham again, but this time by myself at the Rose Bowl. As soon as I started to hear him speak, this time in a frail voice, that same spirit rose up in me. I started to remember about forty years earlier, hearing him speak with such power in his voice. I remembered how I felt such a connection to the whole presentation, the power of his message, and the reaction from the massive crowds. I felt in my spirit that I was supposed go out and spread the great news of salvation and the love of Jesus, but it was only a seed. Like most seeds that do not have constant water and nourishment, the seed lies dormant but doesn't die.

CBS News had an article titled "Graham Packs Rose Bowl" on November 22, 2004.

> More than 80,000 people gathered in the Rose Bowl to hear the Rev. Billy Graham preach on the

> last day of what probably was one of the prominent American evangelist's final crusades.
>
> About 312,500 of the faithful, the curious and the nostalgic attended over the course of the four-day crusade, which marks the 55th anniversary of the Los Angeles revival that propelled Graham to national fame in 1949.

What does God have stirring in your heart and soul?

I had not thought about the feelings I had twice while watching Billy Graham live in 1963 and 2004 until I was listening to the radio, and they announced the passing of Billy Graham on February 21, 2018, at the age of ninety-nine.

As I prayed for his family and friends, I saw a vision of me watching him speak at both venues, as a little kid and then a grown adult. I couldn't remember the dates, but I remembered the locations, so I googled it. When I was reading the news reports of those two crusades, I felt in my heart and soul, "It's time for you to start sharing your message of salvation and the love of Jesus."

I started praying several times a day for clarity of my vision, listening to several messages from Rick Warren, Greg Laurie, Joel Osteen, and Joyce Meyers. I would ask for prayer at my church when our pastor would ask for people to come to the front who felt the message was for them that day. If it had anything to do with writing a book, becoming a disciple for Jesus, or starting a ministry, I was up there asking for prayer and direction.

On Friday, April 19, 2019, a Good Friday, we finally launched i-Praise Internet Church and our www.i-Praise.org website. I recorded my first video message for that Easter, and it was amazing because I was not as nervous as I thought it would be. This happened fourteen months after I had received my vision to start my ministry.

I was so excited to see and hear all the comments and likes about my message and how it touched people. To my disappointment, only twenty people watched it, and there were no comments except from my wife and a couple of friends. I was devasted!

"What happened, Lord? Aren't I following Your Word, the Bible? Did I hear this wrong, Lord? Am I really supposed to do this?" I had all these doubts about the money I had spent on the website, the almost six months adding content and downloads before the site could go live. What had I done?

These doubts and fears were in response to what I felt Satan was telling me and wanting me to believe.

> The thief's [Satan's] purpose is to steal and kill and destroy. My [Jesus's] purpose is to give them a rich and satisfying life. (John 10:10 NLT)

I believe that Satan was trying to stop my ministry before it even got started. "Twenty people. Bob, really?" I thought. "Maybe I didn't hear everything correctly about my ministry, and I need to shut this down before I make a fool of myself and waste any more money and time on this nonsense!"

I prayed about my ministry continuously for days. "Am I supposed to do this, Lord? I do not have the finances to close my business and pursue my ministry full-time, but I feel so happy and content when I'm writing my book and videoing my messages. I feel so fulfilled talking to people about the love of Jesus, Lord. Help me, God!"

In my car, I listen to three stations on XM Satellite Radio: Channel 63, The Massage, which is Christian music; Channel 128, Joel Osteen Radio; and Channel 131, Family Talk. If I am in a car that does not have satellite radio, I listen to The Fish and K-Love Christian on the FM band.

I would hear Joel say, "God didn't put His purpose for your life inside another person. He placed it in your heart. You can't believe the lies the enemy is telling you. Believe in what God says about you!" I would hear these words, and it was like water covering the seed God planted in me.

In Rick Warren's book *The Purpose Driven Life*—(I recommend everyone reads this book)—he says, "True humility is not thinking less of yourself; it is thinking of yourself less." Another quote says, "We are products of our past, but we don't have to be prisoners of it." I would think to myself after reading these quotes, "Am I thinking of others and not myself? I know I have a very sinful past, but God is confirming that I don't have to be a prisoner to it. I do not have to allow Satan into my mind, telling me something different." (please see www.goodreads.com/work/quotes/2265235-the-purpose-driven-life)

Has Satan done that to you when you are trying to show the love of Jesus to others? Do negative things come against you that do not make sense, when all you are trying to do is serve the Lord?

I read a quote from Greg Laurie: "Every disciple is a believer, but not every believer is necessarily a disciple." (please see www.goodreads.com/quotes/742908-every-disciple-is-a-believer)

Barna Research is a Christian research organization where you can find almost ever statistic on Christianity or other religions across America since 1993. A study they have developed and followed since 1993 is about whose responsibility it is to share the Gospel and help bring nonbelievers and prodigals back to Jesus and God. Here is what their survey reports.

> Just 1 in 10 (10%) of the Christians in 1993 who had shared about their faith agreed with the statement "converting people to Christianity is the job of the local church"—as opposed to the job of an individual (i.e., themselves). Twenty-five years later, three in 10 (30%) Christians who have had a conversation about faith say evangelism is the local church's responsibility, a threefold increase. (please see Research releases in Faith &

> Christianity – May 15,2018 www.Barna.com/research/sharing-faith-increasingly)

This is not what the Bible teaches from the Great Commission. We read in Matthew 28:19–20 (NIV),

> Therefore, go and make disciples of all nations, baptizing them in the name of the Father and of the Son and of the Holy Spirit, and teaching them to obey everything I have commanded you. And surely, I am with you always, to the very end of the age.

The Great Commission does not say that it is only to be carried out by pastors, priests, chaplains, or ministers. This is the Great Commission for 100 percent of Christians. It is very simple: if you are a follower of God and believe the Word of God to be true, then this Great Commission is talking to you, to me, and to every one of us.

I hear God speaking to me through the Christian music I listen to, like the songs I have in this book. They help me every day to deepen my relationship with Jesus. The closer my relationship is with God and Jesus, the more they reveal to me. God shows me whether I am on the right path of my ministry and encourages me to keep fighting the good fight against Satan.

How much time are you spending each day to deepen your relationship with God and Jesus?

> Defend the poor and fatherless; Do justice to the afflicted and needy. Deliver the poor and needy; Free them from the hand of the wicked. (Psalm 82:3–4 NKJV)

I am trying my best to be a good disciple of Jesus by obeying God's Word from the Bible and the purpose He placed in my heart. What I learned is that I am a work in progress, and it is not about the number of people I minister to that is important. It is the message each person hears. If God has placed one person or one hundred people in front of me, the message is what is most important.

I recently launch our new community nonprofit called AllLivesMatter2God.org, and I pray we can use the sales of this book and other promotional merchandise to raise money for grassroots community nonprofits that support the poor.

My prayer is that once this book is completed and released, I will be invited to speak at local churches to share my testimony as a prodigal of Jesus and encourage other prodigals to return to the flock and rejoin to the Body of Christ. Amen.

Are you following Jesus and sharing His Great news of salvation and His love for His children, like the Bible instructs us to do? Or are you leaving your responsibility to others?

NOTES

Eight

I Sent You

It took me several years of prayer and signs of confirmation before I mentioned to anyone about my book and my dream.

One day I was driving to work, and I started hearing this song on the radio, "Do Something" by Matthew West. As I learned the words to the song and started singing them, the words got down in my soul. Instead of hearing the words as a song, the words became a message from God to me. We need to stop praying and waiting for some big revelation to move us into our purpose. Take what you have now, the gifts you have now, and God will provide what you do not have. That is what the words to this song mean to me.

I love the song "Do Something" so much, and the message even more. This song is one of our i-Praise Internet Church's theme songs. The other theme song of i-Praise is "Nobody" by Casting Crown, which I mentioned in chapter 1.

This is how I felt when I saw all the hurt in the world, all the poverty in our country, the greatest country on earth with the highest percentage of so-called Christians at over 73 percent of our society, yet it seemed to me like God wasn't doing enough.

I felt like a nobody trying to share my story about my life as a prodigal son and my return to my relationship with Jesus, and I had to "Do Something" to help take care of the poor, the unwanted, the forgotten, the abused, and the mistaken children of God as His servant leader and their provider.

I love to listen to Christian music on Sirius Radio's channel 63, The Message, and K-Love and The Fish on FM ratio. As I learned words and sang the songs, the words got in my soul.

The song talks about a person like me who wakes up one day shouting at the Lord about all the problems in our country and around the world. With the political division, COVID-19, the protests, lootings, killings, and the economic destruction of America, God, You have to send someone to fix it. The song made me feel like I heard, "I did. I created you and have sent you to do your part of the puzzle!"

Wow, did that ever hit home! God created me, and God gave me a road map for how I am supposed to share the greatest news ever reported: That Jesus is our Redeemer and our Guide. That through salvation, we can live a life of peace, joy, blessing, satisfaction, and love. That no matter where we are economically, physically, or emotionally, Jesus is here.

The Prophet Isaiah says in Isaiah 52:7 (ESV),

> How beautiful upon the mountains are the feet of him who brings good news, who publishes peace, who brings good news of happiness, who publishes salvation, who says to Zion, "Your God reigns."

I realized that if we are truly Christians, living out what Jesus taught us and modeled for us during His three-year ministry on earth, we have to be the ones serving the poor. We are the ones who need to rescue the children sold into slavery!

I have learned over my journey back to God and my personal relationship with Jesus that the more we give of what has been given to us, God will bless in ways we could never imagine.

My challenge to everyone reading this book is that you will become more like Jesus. No more telling people what we as Christians think is our duty by telling other nonbelievers and other Christians all about their sins and what they are doing wrong. Instead, we need to stop playing the God of judgment role and get back in our own lane. We need to start doing what Jesus said we are to do while we are on earth.

> So now I am giving you a new commandment: Love each other. Just as I have loved you, you should love each other.(John 13:34 NTL)

That's it, folks! It's simple to say, but it's amazingly hard to do.

People want to be loved and accepted as they are, so if we all want to feel love, why is it so hard to show love?

Do you have someone in your life whom you should be showing the love of Jesus to right now?

I thought to myself, that was the dream God placed in my heart is 2010. I was supposed to use the proceeds of my books, my ministry, and my public speaking events to give back to those in need in America.

How can you "Do Something" like the song says? What gifts and talents has God given you that you can share with others?

It reminds me of the story in the Bible about the master of this company. He was going away for a while, so he called in three of his servants, or employees, and gave them different amounts of money to watch over while he was gone.

> For it will be like a man going on a journey, who called his servants and entrusted to them his property. To one he gave five talents, to another two, to another one, to each according to his ability. Then he went away. He who had received the five talents went at once and traded with them, and he made five talents more. So also he who had the two talents made two talents more. But he who had received the

one talent went and dug in the ground and hid his master's money. Now after a long time the master of those servants came and settled accounts with them. And he who had received the five talents came forward, bringing five talents more, saying, "Master, you delivered to me five talents; here, I have made five talents more." His master said to him, "Well done, good and faithful servant. You have been faithful over a little; I will set you over much. Enter into the joy of your master." And he also who had the two talents came forward, saying, "Master, you delivered to me two talents; here, I have made two talents more." His master said to him, "Well done, good and faithful servant. You have been faithful over a little; I will set you over much. Enter into the joy of your master." He also who had received the one talent came forward, saying, "Master, I knew you to be a hard man, reaping where you did not sow, and gathering where you scattered no seed, so I was afraid, and I went and hid your talent in the ground. Here, you have what is yours." But his master answered him, "You wicked and slothful servant! You knew that I reap where I have not sown and gather where I scattered no seed? Then you ought to have invested my money with the bankers, and at my coming I should have received what was my own with interest. So take the talent from him and give it to him who has the ten talents. For to everyone who has will more be given, and he will have an abundance. But from the one who has not, even what he has will be taken away. And cast the worthless servant into the outer darkness. In that place there will be weeping and gnashing of teeth." (Matthew 25:14–30 ESV)

It is called the parable of the talents, and it says that according to the abilities of each man, one servant received five talents, the second had received two, and the third received only one. The total property entrusted to the three servants was worth eight talents. Now, one talent was worth about twenty years of minimum-labor wages. If we use today's average minimum wage of $20,000 a year times 20 years, it equals $400,000. Five talents would be $2 million, two talents are $800,000, and one talent is $400,000, so these were sizable amounts with which to trust employees. Upon returning home after a long absence, the master asks his three employees for an account of the talents he entrusted to them.

The first and the second servants explain that they each put their talents to work and have doubled the value of the property with which they were entrusted, and each servant was rewarded.

> His master replied, "Well done, good and faithful servant! You have been faithful with a few things; I will put you in charge of many things. Come and share your master's happiness!" (Matthew 25:23 NIV)

But the third man was afraid. He was fearful of what the master would do if he lost the master's money, so he hid it in the ground until the master returned.

> Then the man who had received one bag of gold [Talent] came in. "Master," he said, "I knew that you are a hard man, harvesting where you have not sown and gathering where you have not scattered seed. So, I was afraid and went out and hid your gold [Talent] in the ground. See, here is what belongs to you."

> His master replied, "You wicked, lazy servant! So, you knew that I harvest where I have not sown and gather where I have not scattered seed? Well then, you should have put my money on deposit with the bankers, so that when I returned, I would have received it back with interest.
>
> "So, take the bag of gold [Talent] from him and give it to the one who has ten bags. For whoever has, will be given more, and they will have an abundance. Whoever does not have, even what they have will be taken from them. And throw that worthless employee outside, into the darkness, where there will be weeping and gnashing of teeth." (Matthew 25:24–30 NIV)

Do you have talents God gave you that you can invest in others?

If two hundred million Americans Christians (that's about 73 percent of our population) who say they are Christians would use the talents God gave them to share the love of Jesus across America today, what would America look like?

Do you have a talent for music? Can you donate two hours a week at a battered women's shelter or homeless camp, where you could play some music or teach them music? That's you taking the talent God placed in you, and now you've turned that one talent into ten, twenty, fifty, or one thousand people. Maybe people you are singing to or someone you are teaching finds that God gave them the talent of music, and they start singing to others and teaching them to play the guitar?

What if God gave you the talent as a teacher? Could you find two hours in your week to read or teach reading to other people who cannot read?

What has God blessed you with? Maybe it is a talent for the business of landscaping. Could you see if any of your neighbors are sick or elderly and cannot mow their lawns or pull the weeds? Maybe you could trim the overgrown bushes. Could you spend an hour taking care of others' lawns once a week until they get back on their feet?

What if God gave you the talent to cook? Could you cook some meals and hand them out to the homeless and hungry around your neighborhood?

What if God has blessed you with the talent of running a business with lots of employees? Can you set up a few charity programs your employees can get behind and do fundraisers and donations as a company once a month?

This parable is about using the talents God gives each one of us, no matter how big or small our talents are. We are commissioned to multiply those talents for others to enjoy and prosper with.

Matthew goes on to finish the story, and he writes in Matthew 25:40–45 (NIV),

> The King [Jesus] will reply, "Truly I tell you, whatever you did for one of the least of these brothers and sisters of mine, you did for me."
>
> Then he will say to those on his left, "Depart from me, you who are cursed, into the eternal fire prepared for the devil and his angels. For I was hungry and you gave me nothing to eat, I was thirsty and you gave me nothing to drink, I was a stranger and you did not invite me in, I needed clothes and you did not clothe me, I was sick and in prison and you did not look after me."
>
> They [the so-called followers of Jesus] also will answer, "Lord, when did we see you hungry or thirsty or a stranger or needing clothes or sick or in prison, and did not help you?"

> He will reply, "Truly I tell you, whatever you did not do for one of the least of these, you did not do for me."

Bam—right in our faces! "Whatever you did not do for one of the least of these, you did not do for Me."

This was a call to action for me! This is the verse that slapped me in the head and said, "Wake up, Bob. God gave you so many talents, and what are you doing with them? Whom are you sharing them with? Why are you burying the talents God gave you?"

The song, "Do Something" by Matthew West and this parable in Matthews set my life on a different direction than the direction I thought I was headed.

Is it time for you to stand up and do something?

My prayer is that you will tell people about my book so we can use the profits to do something for the organizations we currently support and have many new opportunities to support other ministries and missions through our i-Praise Internet Church and our community nonprofit, AllLivesMatter2God.org.

I truly believe that we have enough churches in America, but we need more missions in America. What is the difference? Over the last sixty to seventy years, a church building has been known as a place to go every Sunday to worship God and put in our one hour weekly obligation to God. "O God, bless me, my work, my family, my finances, and my health for the next 168 hours (one week). After all, I just gave you one hour of my time that I could have been home watching sports, working in the yard, or going for a bike ride. But no, God—I gave that one special hour to You."

> The King will reply, "Truly I tell you, whatever you did for one of the least of these brothers and sisters of mine, you did for me." (Matthew 25:40 NIV)

Close your eyes and think about what you see when you think of going to a mission. Wikidiff.com writes, "The difference between mission and church is that a mission is a set of tasks that fulfills a purpose or duty; an assignment set by an employer while church is a Christian house of worship; a building where religious services take place."

The History Channel's website explains what life was like in a traditional California mission in the late 1700s and early 1800s.

> The missions created new communities where the Native Americans received religious education and instruction. The Spanish established pueblos (towns) and presidios (forts) for protection.
>
> The natives lived in the missions until their religious training was complete. Then, they would move to homes outside of the missions (House churches).
>
> Once the natives converted to Christianity, the missionaries would move on to new locations, and the existing missions served as churches.
>
> The native converts were known as "neophytes." After they were baptized, they were expected to perform labor. Typically, men worked in the fields, and women cooked. Both learned Spanish and attended church.
>
> Farming was an especially important job in the mission community. Wheat, barley, and maize were some of the staple crops that were grown. The Spanish missionaries also brought fruits from Europe, such as apples, peaches, and pears.

> Other jobs included carpentry, building, weaving and leather-working.

I believe we need to turn churches into missions for the local communities. I believe we have too many physical buildings and not enough missions. In America, we call them rescue missions.

I believe we need to focus on building Christian rescue missions across America where people can go when they need food. A mission is a place people can go and be trained to work in an industry that can pay them a living wage, and it is a place for shelter while the people are getting back on their feet.

There is plenty of food and clothing for the poor and the homeless. What they need is mental health care, job training, jobs, and safe housing.

Our job as Christians, believers, followers, and disciples of Jesus should be to serve the ones Jesus taught us to serve.

When I read my Bible, I do not read very much about all the time Jesus spent at the synagogues (churches in the Jewish faith). Almost all of what I read is Jesus healing the sick, feeding the poor, and helping the least of His society. I read about Him teaching and modeling for us God's love through Jesus.

Why do we feel we can call ourselves followers of Jesus, but we are not following Jesus's example? How can we say we are Christlike when we don't act like Christ?

Remember the Words of Jesus: "Whatever you do for the least of these, you do for me also, says Jesus."

Do you need to repent and ask Jesus to forgive you for not using the talents God gave you, especially since Jesus showed you how to use them? Now is the best time to bow your head, ask for forgiveness, and ask for a clear direction to use your talents to serve others.

NOTES

Nine

God's Image Revealed

As I have been walking with God and with Jesus, God has revealed Himself to me is so many ways, I know He is real, and I know the Bible is the truth.

We have all seen the signs the guys hold up in the end zones of football games or other sporting events.

> For God so loved the world that he gave his one and only Son, that whoever believes in him shall not perish but have eternal life. (John 3:16 NIV)

I want us to look at the verse after and a couple of verses before the famous verse of John 3:16.

> Just as Moses lifted up the snake in the wilderness, so the Son of Man must be lifted up, that everyone who believes may have eternal life in him.
>
> For God so loved the world that he gave his one and only Son, that whoever believes in him shall not perish but have eternal life. For God did not send

> his Son into the world to condemn the world, but to save the world through him. (John 3:14–17 NIV)

"The Son of Man must be lifted up"—this is Jesus whom John is talking about. We must lift up the name of Jesus in our families, our friends, our neighborhoods, our community, and our country.

Who is supposed to doing the lifting? We are to do the lifting in the name of Jesus. Not just the local pastor or priest or the local church building. The followers of Jesus should also do the lifting.

Have you ever tried to lift up something heavy, and if you try by yourself, it is impossible? When you get one more person, it is still hard, but you can lift it up a little bit. When you get four people to help do the lifting, it is not heavy at all; you can lift it up and down like it is nothing. Why? Because we are better together. We get more done as a team instead of as individuals.

One person in one day may be able to share the great news of salvation and show the love of Jesus to two or three people on a good day. But what if ten people shared the great news, and those ten people showed the love of Jesus? Now they have touched twenty to thirty people in a day. What if we have one thousand people sharing the great news and showing the love of Jesus? Now they have touched two to three thousand people in one day!

What if 200 million followers—the 73 percent of Americans who claim to be Christians—lifted up the name of Jesus to two to three people apiece? Around 500 million people would be able to see the love of Jesus. The US population is only about 330 million people, so some would receive two or three blessings and would see the love of Jesus.

What would life be like in America?

All we are asked to do is share the great news of salvation: that if we repent of our sins, ask Jesus into our lives, believe in what the Bible teaches and that Jesus rose from the grave, and we surrender our hearts, minds, and souls to serving Jesus, we will live in heaven for eternity.

Let me ask you a question. If you had the cure for cancer, and by telling others you could save their lives, would you tell them? If you had a cure for COVID 19, and all you needed to do was to tell people how they could be cured, would you tell them?

We have been given a prescription and a cure to the sickness of fear, depression, unhappiness, discouragement, any illnesses we might have, lack of finances, concern over our children, and the feeling of isolation. All these sicknesses have a cure, and you have the prescription for the cure. His name is Jesus Christ.

Do not be afraid to talk to someone about Jesus. Tell others your testimony; God made sure we all have one.

As I have leaned into God more and walked in a much closer relationship with Jesus, He has revealed more and more of Himself to me.

I remember in 1996, right before I recommitted my life back to God and Jesus, I was sitting in my car at the park by my house and thinking about driving off the side of the road and into the canyon, committing suicide. I felt so lost and overwhelmed with my life that this seemed like the best thing for everyone. God revealed Himself to me down in my spirit, and I felt I needed to go to Saddleback Church so I could meet Him there.

I started up my car, drove to Saddleback Church, and walked to an area by the sanctuary I call my prayer garden. I would stop by Saddleback sometimes on my way home, go to the bench by this garden area, and talk to God and Jesus. On Wednesday, they had Walk and Worship, so I tried to make that each week.

But that night, when I heard from God down in my spirit, I sat down on the bench at the prayer garden and could immediately feel the presence of Jesus. I sat there crying and telling Jesus how confused I was and how I just wanted all the problems to go away. I had rubbed my Jesus genie bottle, yet Jesus did not magically appear and take away all my troubles. This was a feeling I had in my spirit. I should follow God's Word and give God my burdens, and He would make them light.

> Come to me, all who labor and are heavy laden, and I will give you rest. Take my yoke upon you, and learn from me, for I am gentle and lowly in heart, and you will find rest for your souls. For my yoke is easy, and my burden is light. (Matthew 11:28–30 ESV)

I thought, "Oh, wow, Lord, is that really You?"

I immediately started feeling better. If you remember back a couple of chapters, I was sharing the story about Peter walking on the water, but when he saw the wind, he was scared, lost his faith, and started sinking. What did Jesus do? He immediately reached out His hand and helped Peter back into the boat to safety.

I gave each of my concerns and worries one at a time to Jesus. I prayed over one concern and thanked God for removing that concern, and then I would go to the next concern. After about a half hour, I started feeling each concern lift off me. I could think more clearly even though I still was not sure how things would end up.

Jesus immediately reached out His hand, and He took my hand. We have walked hand in hand ever since.

I remembered in the Bible where it says to not be anxious for anything. It has become one of my favorite promises of Jesus, and I have it posted on the wall in my office.

> Do not be anxious about anything, but in every situation, by prayer and petition, with thanksgiving, present your requests to God. And the peace of God, which transcends all understanding, will guard your hearts and minds in Christ Jesus. (Philippians 4:6–7 NIV)

I am not good at memorizing Bible verses or anything except music. I can still hear a song that I have not heard for thirty years, yet I can remember most of the words and even the drumbeats and guitar licks. This is the reason why in each chapter of this book, I talk about songs and the words that have made their way into my heart and soul. I can sing these songs and their words over and over so they get down in my soul and clear my mind.

The song "Way Maker" is being sung everywhere across America.

The lyrics go, "You are here, moving in our midst."

I finally realized that as long as I wanted to spend time in worshiping Jesus, praying to Jesus, and praising and thanking Jesus, I could feel Him right with me, moving all around me.

The song is saying that God is with us, making His presence felt in us and in the place we are at.

The words of the song are telling us who God is. God makes a way in the desert; He is the Way Maker. He gives sight to the blind, raises people from the dead, heals the sick, and feeds five thousand men plus women and children with two fish and five loaves of bread. He is the Miracle Maker. Jesus is perfect, and His promises are never broken; He is the Promise Keeper. Jesus teaches us that He is the light of the world, and we need to shine His light in the darkness in and around our lives; He is the light in the darkness. That is who our God is! Amen and amen.

God and Jesus are present everywhere, touching our hearts, healing our hearts, and turning around lost lives like He turned my life around. He is mending all the hurts to our hearts. In return for those blessings, "I worship You, Jesus, I worship You."

Has Jesus turned your life around? Are you praising and worshiping His name?

Our God and Jesus are all of the following things.

> **Way Maker**—For I'm going to do a brand-new thing. See, I have already begun! Don't you see it? I will make a road through the wilderness of the world for my people to go home, and create rivers for them in the desert! (Isaiah 43:19 TLB)

> **Miracle Worker**—By faith in the name of Jesus, this man whom you see and know was made strong. It is Jesus' name and the faith that comes through him that has completely healed him, as you can all see. (Acts 3:16 NIV)
>
> **Promise Keeper**—So, do not fear, for I am with you; do not be dismayed, for I am your God. I will strengthen you and help you; I will uphold you with my righteous right hand. (Isaiah 41:10 NIV)
>
> **Light in the Darkness**—When Jesus spoke again to the people, he said, "I am the light of the world. Whoever follows me will never walk in darkness but will have the light of life." (John 8:12 NIV)

I encourage you to listen to "Way Maker" over and over. Whenever you are questioning God and Jesus—and we all do at times—you can sing it out and get your spirit in line with who God is and the peace He can bring to us.

We own a food equipment consulting company here in Southern California, and like any small business, cash flow is always needed and not readily available, so it can test our faith.

I used to grab my Jesus genie bottle every time there was a problem: a bill coming due and no money to pay it, payroll is due, and others are depending on me to provide them paychecks. I would rub and rub, hoping that Jesus would pop out and fix my situation. I learned that Jesus is not a genie, He is always present, always in our midst, and He reveals it at the most opportune times and not our time.

I remember one day I was at home going through my morning devotion and asking God for some sales. I decided to drive to my office and pray there. I was never much for praying on my knees even though the Bible says we should pray on our knees.

> For this reason I bow my knees before the Father, from whom every family in heaven and on earth is named, that according to the riches of his glory he may grant you to be strengthened with power through his Spirit in your inner being, so that Christ may dwell in your hearts through faith—that you, being rooted and grounded in love, may have strength to comprehend with all the saints what is the breadth and length and height and depth. (Ephesians 3:14–21 ESV)

I arrive at the office before anyone arrived, and I first listened to Jeremy Riddle singing "O Hail King Jesus," one of my favorite songs before my morning devotions. After the song was over and I was down on my knees for the whole song, head and arms raised, I started to pray. I asked God for four specific blessings over our business. Now, it is scary when you pray for specific results, but you will be amazed at how God steps in and answers prayers specifically. Does this happen 100 percent when I pray a specific prayer now? No. In fact, it does not happen very often at all. Why? Because we do not know the best path in our maze to reach our purpose, but God does.

In the Bible, Jesus teaches His disciples to pray in Matthew 6:10 (ESV): "Your kingdom come, your will be done, on earth as it is in heaven."

"His will be done"—not Bob's will be done. Many Christians, like me, turn our backs on Jesus and God, and we turn away from going to church when our specific prayers are not met, when we expect them to be met, so it is God's fault. Don't let Satan and his demons make you think that when people at church prayed for healing for you and you didn't get healed, the people at the church must be a bunch of fakes!

Satan gets in our minds, and we need to stay in God's presence so He can keep Satan out.

I prayed these four specific things:

(1) I needed more quote requests from our website for the machines we sell and service. We were averaging about one every two months.

(2) A sale to close from a specific meat processor.

(3) Money that we were owed for several months would come into the business.

(4) One of my salesman would turn in a sale.

I got up from my knees and went to my desk to turn on my computer for the day. When I opened my email, I saw two quote requests for machines. Never had we had two in one day before today. I was reading emails, and a new email popped in from one of my salesmen. He said, "Bob, you are not going to believe this, but a company just contacted me and said they had changed their minds, and they are ordering one of the machines immediately, with the other coming in 2020." This same company had contacted him a few days earlier and said the owners had decided not to move forward purchasing the machines. But now they had changed their minds—or did God soften their hearts? About an hour later, I got an email from a customer that said he was sending in his past due payment and was ordering another machine, and he wanted to pay us in advance.

My team arrived at work, and I could not wait to tell them the news about how three of my four prayer requests were answered exactly how I had prayed. They were so excited, and we thanked God for the blessing. We were extremely happy with three out of four prayers being answered, but God is a God of completion. About three hours into our day, another customer to whom I had emailed a quote regarding a machine several months earlier called and said he was ready to order the machine! Four out of four, baby! As the song says, "Our God is an awesome God!" Yes, He is. Amen!

Many of our business associates, vendors, and clients know I am a Christian, and everyone who works here are also Christians. When I told them my exciting story about all my prayers being answered, they were amazed. I had good conversations about those miracles with several people, and it helps others to believe that God can do miracles for them as well.

If you want to feel God's presence, then you must be present with Him. You cannot simply grab your Jesus genie bottle anytime you need a blessing and expect it to be answered. But if you are constantly in God's presence, you will start to recognize when God is talking to you. You must be still and open. Do not do all the talking. Make your request known and then wait on the answer.

Understand that God and Jesus are always present with us and in us, but not everything we ask for is good for us in our journey. No matter how much you beg and plead, no matter how hard you rub the Jesus genie bottle, if your prayer does not lead you to your purpose God placed you on earth to accomplish, He will not answer that prayer.

I used the example of a hedge maze in an earlier chapter. We wander through this maze we call life, and because we cannot see where God is leading us, we run into roadblocks. Instead of asking for God's presence to guide us through the maze, we go in the wrong direction and run into dead ends. Because He is above the maze, He can guide us through the obstacles. When we make another wrong turn, we simply need to look up to Jesus, and He will get us heading in the right direction.

We can run through the maze of life getting more and more anxious and uneasy, and we start losing our faith that we will get through the maze alive, unharmed, and safe.

Peter was in the maze, so to speak, not knowing what to do or where to go. Jesus immediately reached out His hand, and Peter was saved. Peter believed so much in what Jesus told him to do, Peter was a part of the miracle. But when Peter lost faith, he started to sink, and he missed his full blessing. Think of how much fun Peter could have had if he had simply stayed in faith.

Peter could have been running on top of the water, waving to the rest of the disciples as they sat afraid in the boat, but instead he lost his faith, and he lost his blessing.

Are you in a storm right now? Will you stay in faith and take hold of Jesus's hand so He can get you safely through the storm you're in, or will you lose your faith and miss the full blessing God has in store for each and every one of us?

NOTES

Ten

How Great Is Our God

We Christians believe in the Triune God, or the Trinity. There is one God, or what some call, The Source, and out of God is the Father (in heaven), the Son (Jesus the man), and the Holy Spirit (who lives within us and fills us up).

> The amazing grace of the Master, Jesus Christ, the extravagant love of God, the intimate friendship of the Holy Spirit, be with all of you. (2 Corinthians 13:14 MSG)

I like this translation of this scripture because of the adjectives the writer is using, amazing grace, extravagant love, intimate friendship.

God makes these promises to everybody, not just Christians. Remember, "For God so Love the *world*, that He Gave His only Son" (John 3:16 NIV).

We need to accept God, Jesus and the Holy Spirit into our heart and lives to receive God's promises.

These are promises from the God of the universe, the Source of all that we are, we see, we touch, we smell, we eat, we hear, we feel—everything. If I believe, as a Christian, that God is everywhere and is everything that is good, then I must believe in His Word, the Bible.

The Bible is the inspired Word of God, passed down through prophets, Jesus, and the disciples, for God's children to follow. It should be taught to us and embraced deep within us, as our Road map through this maze of life.

> The whole Bible was given to us by inspiration from God and is useful to teach us what is true and to make us realize what is wrong in our lives; it straightens us out and helps us do what is right. It is God's way of making us well prepared at every point, fully equipped to do good to everyone. (2 Timothy 3:16–17 TLB)

This is another scripture, or love letter, from God, showing His children all the great plans, gifts, and adventures God has for us.

> This is how we know we're living steadily and deeply in him, and he in us: He's given us life from his life, from his very own Spirit. Also, we've seen for ourselves and continue to state openly that the Father sent his Son as Savior of the world. Everyone who confesses that Jesus is God's Son, participates continuously in an intimate relationship with God. We know it so well, we've embraced it heart and soul, this love that comes from God. (1 John 4:16 MSG)

God's Word is our shield of protection against the flaming arrows from the enemy, Satan, the devil, the liar, the deceiver, the destroyer—whatever you want to call him.

The Bible says in 1 Corinthians 10:13 (TLB),

> But remember this—the wrong desires that come into your life aren't anything new and different.

> Many others have faced exactly the same problems before you. And no temptation is irresistible. You can trust God to keep the temptation from becoming so strong that you can't stand up against it, for he has promised this and will do what he says. He will show you how to escape temptation's power so that you can bear up patiently against it.

Remember that the temptation itself is not a sin unless you act upon the temptation. Then it becomes a sin.

With every promise from God comes participation from us. You cannot simply pray away a problem—you must act on it. You first pray and mediate on the problem. Be still and see whether you are getting any feeling inside, an intuition, a random thought that might not make sense at the time. You must come up with a plan in partnership with God through the words He will give to you.

You might be like me and receive God's message in dreams or visions. Here is a vision I want to share with you. I had a vision of me working in a mission feeding people while I was driving down the freeway in Anaheim, and it was so weird because the vision didn't impair my vision of the road and traffic.

Here is another story about God giving me a nudge or feeling inside. I was driving to work in Los Angeles from Orange, where I lived. It was about 5:30 a.m., and this day I went a different route to the freeway. I do not remember whether there was a specific reason, like an accident I wanted to avoid, but I felt like I was supposed to drive this route this morning. As I came to the red left turn signal, I saw this homeless man walking across the street in the crosswalk, and I felt in my spirit that the Lord wanted me to give him some water and pray for him. I said, "Lord, I am turning left, and he will be on the far right side of the street. I cannot cut over to the far right because there are cars in those lanes already." I felt the Lord give me another nudge, so the light turned green, and I turned left, still thinking about this guy and my water. I always carried two bottles of water because it was a long drive to my office. My turn to the freeway was the far right lane, but instead I drove straight until I could make a legal U-turn.

About five minutes had passed since the man had crossed the street and was walking east. I said to God, "It's been a while, Lord, but if You want me to give this man water and pray for him, You need to help me find him." The funny thing was this man had many options for directions to go, but God guided my car right to the man. It was amazing.

I pulled up to the man and rolled down my window to talk to him. I said, "Good morning," and he replied the same. I said, "The Lord told me to find you, give you this bottle of water, and pray for you.

This is where the goose bumps happen. The man says to me, "You might not believe this, but as I was walking up to the light to cross the street, I felt a deep thirst for water." He said he did not have any water with him, and he asked God to send him water. Therefore, me pulling up and offering him a bottle of water was an answer to his prayer, and it amazed both of us. We prayed and praised together and introduced ourselves. Before I left, he said the water was great, but a hot cup of coffee would be an answer to a prayer as well. I parked my car, we walked over to a gas station, and I bought him a cup of coffee. Two answers to prayers, two miracles in less than fifteen minutes for this man whom most look down at or do not see at all as he walks down the street with his worldly possessions in a shopping cart.

How does God speak to you?

The Bible tell us He promises to give us amazing grace, extravagant love, and intimate friendship, but our action or our lack of action will determine whether we receive the promise.

Do you get what I am saying?

Our actions are believing God, through our faith, is who the Bible says He is. We ask for forgiveness of our sins, ask Jesus to be our Lord and Savior, and promise to follow Jesus and His teachings.

If we do this, the Bible says we are born again and will spend eternity in heaven with God and Jesus, as well as all our born-again friends and family.

Once we have received the greatest gift anyone could ever receive, we have to learn what we have to do so we can uphold our end of the promise, which is to follow Jesus and the Word for the rest of our lives.

Do not worry; I am getting to the song real soon. But this is important for me to make sure that I am very clear how following Jesus works. To be honest, I don't see 72 percent of Americans acting very Christlike. My prayer is that you will read this book, God will light a fire in you to change your current behaviors, and we will all start showing the love of Jesus. Stop telling everyone what you are against and start showing them what you are for. Amen.

Now to this song I love so much, "Great Are You, Lord" by Casting Crowns.

It first talks about God giving us life, and it says that God is love, that He is the light of the dark world.

The song talks about how God is the God of hope, and He restores us. There is nothing greater than our God.

> Because Your loving kindness is better than life, My lips shall praise You. (Psalm 63:3 NKJV)
>
> Your word is a lamp to my feet and a light to my path. (Psalm 119:105 NKJV)
>
> The Lord is close to those whose hearts are breaking; he rescues those who are humbly sorry for their sins. (Psalm 34:18 TLB)

Now, this is our action to these promises: we praise God. "Great are You, Lord." We get up in the morning. "Thank You, Lord, for this day You have given me. May Your Will be done through me today. Amen." We praise God's name. "Thank You, Lord for protecting my kids today as they leave this home. Bring them back home safe and sound. Amen." We are driving to work and listening to worship music on the radio, praising God's name in singing.

We go to lunch, and before we eat, we say, "Thank You, Lord, for the food I'm about to eat. Let it give me nourishment to fulfill Your purpose in my life. Amen." We are in our car, and we turn on XM Family Life radio and listen to Rick Warren's show, *Pastor Rick's Daily Hope*. We pray, "Thank You, Lord, for the words you have given Pastor Rick to speak to me today."

We drive home and listen to the message on XM Radio, such as Joel Osteen Radio, to inspire us to be the best person we can be around our jobs, our partners, our kids, and our neighbors. We listen and worship to more Christian music like Casting Crowns and others, praising God's name.

When we get home and sit down for dinner as a family, we must thank God for the meal and for bringing our family home safe.

Before we go to sleep, we must thank God for the day He gave us and the blessings He gave us that day. We ask God to reveal more of Him to us while we are still and sleeping. The next day, we start all over, praising God's name throughout the day. You find a good parking spot: "Thank You, Lord." Traffic is light: "Thank You, Lord." The boss was nice to you today: after you pick yourself off the floor, "Thank You, Lord!"

We must humble ourselves before God and then praise His name so we can receive His promises and blessings. Amen!

The Bible says in Job 33:4 (NKJV),

> The Spirit of God has made me, and the breath of the Almighty gives me life.

Because God gives us our breath every day, like the song says, "we pour out our praise to You only."

We all tend to take credit when things are going right in our lives. We just got a promotion we have been praying about. We take our family out to dinner to celebrate, and as we are explaining the events of the meeting, we start to highlight all that we did to earn the promotion. By the end of the evening, we never thanked or praised God even though it was He who gave us that promotion.

What if any of us were driving and we get into a bad accident and wreck our car on the freeway. We immediately grab the Jesus genie bottle out of the glovebox we have had Him in since the last disaster, and we start rubbing away. "Jesus, get me out of the mess. Jesus, You are our Savior—fix this now!" I'm sorry but Jesus is not a genie.

Have you walked away from God and Jesus like I did over twenty-four years ago? Do you need to return to His promises and His love? Have you been a Sunday Christian, giving God just one hour a week as an obligation to go to church, but you are not engaged?

Pew research mentions that 40 percent of Christians say they do not feel the presence of God when they are in church. Do you feel His presence?

Maybe it is time that you spent more time with your heavenly Father—starting today.

To feel His presence, we must be present first. Are you present with God, or are you only present when you need to rub the Jesus genie bottle?

Remember, Jesus is not a genie!

God bless.

Big Jesus hugs.

NOTES

CLOSING

If you enjoyed my book, "Jesus Is Not A Genie" *My Story: The Prodigal Son Returns,* I pray that you tell your family and friends so they can pick up a copy for themselves.

If you want to know more about my ministry, i-Praise Internet Church, you can check out our website, www.i-Praise.org for blogs, messages, music, and the ministries we support.

If we can help with your journey with Jesus, please contact me through the i-Praise website under "Comments," and it will go directly to my email address.

You can also check out our community religious nonprofit, All Lives Matter 2 God, at AllLivesMatter2God.org.

If you want to recommit your life back to Jesus, or you would like to receive Jesus for the first time, simply pray with me: "Lord Jesus, I repent of my sins. Please come into my life every day and every hour, Father. I believe in the Father, the Son, and the Holy Spirit, and I want to follow You, Jesus, every day of my life until I can join You in heaven. Amen!"

If you prayed that prayer, we believe you've been born again, and we would love to help you find a good Bible-based church in your area.

You are always welcome to join us on our i-Praise Internet Church Facebook group. Our group started on Easter weekend 2019 with five people, and as of this writing we have over 1,500 people following i-Praise on Facebook. Thank You, Lord, for Your blessing and goodness to i-Praise and the i-Praise family.

God's dream to me wasn't to write one book and then fade into the sunset. God placed a dream in me that I would write a series of books. My prayer is that I will write a series of Jesus Is Not a Genie books on several subjects and several groups of people.

Check out our Jesus Is Not a Genie website at Jesusisnotagenie.org.

ABOUT THE AUTHOR

Bob Maxwell is a small business owner in Southern California. Bob left the church and God when he was 17 years old only and return to God and the church in 1995. Bob has since launched an Internet Church called I-Praise Internet Church (www.i-Praise.org) where Bob minister's to people that traditionally don't attend a traditional church. Bob also has an I-Praise Group Facebook page which has over 1,500 Followers.

Printed in the United States
By Bookmasters